HAPPINESS AND CONTEMPLATION

*Contemplation does not rest until it
has found the object which dazzles it.*

KONRAD WEISS

JOSEF PIEPER

Happiness

AND

Contemplation

Introduced by
Ralph McInerny

Translated by
Richard and Clara Winston

St. Augustine's Press
South Bend, Indiana
1998

Original German title: *Glück und Kontemplation* from Kösel-Verlag, Mönchen

Manufactured in the United States of America.

2 3 4 5 6 05 04 03 02 01

Library of Congress Cataloging in Publication Data
Pieper, Josef, 1904-
    [Glück und Kontemplation. English]
    Happiness and contemplation / Josef Pieper : introduced by Ralph McInerny ; translated by Richard and Clara Winston.
          p.   cm.
    Originally published: New York : Pantheon, c1958. With new introd.
    Includes bibliographical references (p.)
    ISBN 1-890318-30-2 (cloth : alk. paper). – ISBN 1-890318-31-0 (pbk. : alk. paper)
    1. Contemplation. 2. Happiness. I. Title.
    BV5091.C7P513 1998
    248.3'4—dc21   98-18476
                                         CIP

∞*The paper used in this publication meets the minimum requirements of the American National Standard for Information Sciences—Permanence of Paper for Printed Materials, ANSI Z39.48-1984.*

CONTENTS

The finite spirit is by virtue of his nature
insatiable—unless he partake of God Himself.

V

Happiness and joy are two different things. Joy is
essentially secondary, the response to happiness. The
goods which we seek even at the cost of joy.
Nevertheless joy has no purpose beyond itself.

VI

Happiness means: attaining "the whole good." But what
is meant by "attaining"? Happiness as a result of acting
and doing. Three fundamental propositions: happiness
mean perfection; perfection means realization;
realization comes by acting. Acting that remains within.
The work does not absorb the creator.

VII

The wholly happy man is one who sees. The opposing
argument: Do we love in order to know? Knowing as
the "noblest form of possession." Augustine, too, says,
"Our whole reward is seeing." Possession of the beloved
object is knowing it. "This is the Eternal Life."

VIII

The two modes of the act of love: longing and joy. "To
know" in the Biblical sense: closest presence. Happy is
the man who sees what he loves. "Where love is, there is
the eye too." Contemplation as awareness of the beloved
object.

IX

What constitutes contemplation? First: silent perception
of reality. Second: not thinking, but intuition; intuition
is knowledge of what is present. Third: knowing

accompanied by amazement. Only one who does not see
the whole can be amazed.

X

Earthly contemplation based on the premise that
"intuition" is possible for physical man also, and that he
can somehow comprehend the "drink called
happiness." There is no nonreligious contemplation.
But awareness of the divine element can be kindled by
virtually anything encountered. The obscure and
simultaneously commonplace forms of contemplation
and the need that they may be recognized for what they
are. Gerard Manley Hopkins. The message experienced
by intuition is not communicable. *Page 76*

XI

Reply to the counterarguments of the practical man: In
what does life itself consist once the means of livelihood
have been won? Morality points beyond itself. Loving
means: to desire the beloved to be happy; and
happiness is intuition. It is not possible to rest ultimately
content in the felicity of the active life. Contemplation as
the goal of politics. Practice becomes meaningless as
soon as it is thought to be an end in itself. The
"practice" of the artist: "When something is finished, it
must be perfect—but what then?" Is desiring-to-possess
more than possession? Is joy more important than its
reason? Anaxagoras: We are born for seeing. *Page 89*

XII

The same characteristics are to be found in the intuitive
and the happy man. Simplicity. The step out of time.
Seeing in itself makes for happiness. The closed sphere.
Freedom from fetters. George Santayana: crowning in
intuition. *Page 100*

Happiness and Contemplation

XIII

Ought the high-minded person renounce the "escape of happiness"? Refusal of consent to the world. It is not our merit that the possibility of happiness exists. The "dark night" on the way of contemplation. The sight of the "historical Gethsemane." Happiness founded on sorrow. Its blessing and dazzling light. *Page 105*

Introduction

One need not be a philosopher to wonder what it all means but perhaps only a philosopher would suggest that our deepest longing is for contemplation. It is the major merit of Josef Pieper's *Happiness and Contemplation* that he makes this surprising claim seem like sweet reason itself. As it is.

The opening line of Aristotle's *Metaphysics* is this: "All men by nature desire to know." This will not seem like the first thought that would pop into your mind down at McDonald's or in Row 12 of a boxing match. Remembering some of our relatives might seem to render Aristotle's claim a bad joke. Indeed we might wonder if it covers even ourselves. Yet his is an unqualifiedly universal claim. To be a human being is to want to know.

Aristotle, as it happens, is a great deal of help in understanding how it is that human destiny resides in contemplation of the divine. He follows that opening sentence with the following support for it. "A sign of this is the delight we take in our senses, particularly the sense of sight." Obviously, if taking a look counts as knowing, the claim that everyone wants to know does seem fairly obvious. The opening chapters of Aristotle's *Metaphysics* go on to provide us with a panorama of modes of knowing, leading us by the hand from sense perception, through memory and imagination, through the mastery of the experienced person, on to practical knowledge, and beyond. The common thread that emerges is the desire to know why things happen as they do.

Why? There are all sorts of answer to that question, but some are more comprehensive than others. And the question itself can become all-comprehensive. Why is there anything at all rather than nothing? The delight we take in our senses is an implicit desire to know the ultimate reason for things, the highest cause. The desire for wisdom that philosophy eytmologically is is a desire for the highest or divine causes. Philosophy culminates in theology. All other knowledge contains the seeds of contemplation of the divine.

Of course most people are so caught up in everyday activities that it seems silly to think they will end up contemplating the divine. The philosopher has trouble avoiding the charge of elitism. Aristotle may not have begun by saying that only some men naturally desire to know, but the upshot of the analysis would seem to be that very few indeed ever win through to what he has set down as the very point of human life, contemplation.

Philosophers may have answers to such difficulties, but the answers do not fully satisfy. But then for a thinker like Josef Pieper, philosophy is never the last word.

The contemplation of the philosopher, even if achieved, is an imperfect thing. That is, in the event it always falls short of the goal being pursued. It is fitful, episodic, incomplete. This was something of which the philosophers themselves were sadly aware. What pagans could not know is that there is something undreamt of by philosophers.

The perfect contemplation that is our true destiny is offered to everyone. Every human being without exception is called to an eternal contemplative happiness with God. Access to it is not subject to what Kierkegaard called the differential of natural talent. Christianity suggests that the last will be first and the first last. There is a transvaluation of talents because grace is the decisive motor.

It is the mark of the kind of philosopher Josef Pieper is that references to the world of faith and revelation come naturally to him. He refuses to adopt the secularized persona that has characterized too many modern philosophers. Even if philosophers are themselves religious believers, this is a well-kept secret when they are operating professionally. It is mystifying why this should be so. It is not so for Josef Pieper.

Not that Pieper confuses a philosophical argument with a theological one. He does not expect a reader without the faith to assent to inferences he makes from revealed truths. But these truths form the ambience within which he fashions philosophical arguments. That is the ambience in which Western culture developed, including until recently philosophy. Far from being an impediment to philosophizing, it is a practical condition of doing it well. Among his many contributions, this may be Josef Pieper's greatest. He has shown how much better philosophy is when pursued within the ambience of the faith.

Ralph McInerny
University of Notre Dame

I

With what a multitude of meanings do people speak of happiness. They wish it to one another on weddings and birthdays, at partings, on the first day of the year. The entertainment industry purveys to its "consumers," readers, spectators, and listeners, innumerable stories of happiness threatened, crossed, and at last achieved. Popular songs authoritatively inform every girl what it means to make a man happy. The word crops up in the already somewhat old-fashioned formula of the "greatest happiness for the greatest number," and in manifestoes proclaiming everyone's right to happiness.[1] Anyone cognizant of this welter of possibilities may be extremely surprised to come upon the bald statement that man's ultimate happiness consists in contemplation.

This statement precisely is what we are here concerned with.

It contains a whole philosophy of life, a basic conception of the nature of man and the meaning of human existence.

It is of no special importance that the statement

derives from a book by St. Thomas, his *Summa* against the pagans.[2] Of far greater importance is the fact that this idea belongs to a store of traditional wisdom whose root goes deeper than historical time, and perhaps further than the human domain. If in these pages we frequently cite Thomas Aquinas, we do not mean him to speak primarily for himself. He is intended as the witness for that tradition—though, to be sure, a witness of extraordinary rank. Nor is our study in the main concerned with historical aspects. Rather, our concern is with the light that statement casts upon the reality we encounter, and upon the reality which we are ourselves.

We ought not too soon discard our surprise at the proposition that contemplation is man's ultimate happiness—ought not dismiss it, say, by deciding that happiness is meant here in some special sense which has nothing in common with everyday language. For those words were written with a view to all, even the most trivial meanings of happiness. Ambiguity, and even a tendency to banality, are, it would seem, inherent in the subject itself. These equivocations are to be found in all the languages of men.

The Greek tongue, it must be noted, makes a

unique distinction which lends enormous range to the spectrum of meanings of the word "happiness." For there is a Greek word which denotes exclusively the happiness of the gods: only the gods are *mákares*. But the derivative word *makários*, which basically should denote men's share in the untrammelled happiness of the gods, took on such a vulgar meaning in colloquial Greek that the poets Aeschylus and Sophocles scrupulously avoid it. The second Greek word, *eudaimon*, as used in ordinary speech means the man who has money, although originally it referred to the guidance of man's guardian spirit and hence to the supernatural source of happiness. Incidentally, the Greek New Testament does not once use the words *eudaimon*, *eudaimonia*; in the Beatitudes and elsewhere *makários*, *makariótes* alone are employed. Likewise, in the Vulgate the words *felix* and *felicitas* do not occur, only the parallel words *beatus* and *beatitudo*.[3] But as used in colloquial Latin, even these more spiritual epithets may mean anything from the bliss of God to the *beatus ille homo, qui sedet in sua domo, qui sedet post fornacem.* (Blessed the man who sits in his house, who sits by his fireside.) We may think to avoid such ambiguities by opposing "happiness" to "bliss" or "beatitude." The latter word, it is true, signifies strictly an ultimate state that is not encountered in ordinary life. But the same distinction also exists for *beatitudo* and *makariótes*. In actual usage "bliss" is no more immune than were the Latin and Greek words to debasement, to shallowness, coarseness, and banality.

There is nevertheless a fundamental significance, which should never be overlooked, in the very fact that a single word, "happiness," comprehends such a variety of meanings: the immortal richness of divine life and man's part in it, as well as the petty satisfaction of a fleeting desire. We venture to assert that this ambiguity reflects the structure of the whole of Creation. St. Thomas put it this way: "As created good is a reflection of the uncreated good, so the attainment of a created good is a reflected beatitude."[4]

Now the "attainment of a created good" is a thing that happens constantly, and in a thousand varied forms. It happens whenever a thirsty man drinks, whenever a questioner receives a flash of illumination, whenever lovers are together, whenever a task is brought to a successful conclusion and a plan bears fruit. And when men call all this "happiness," they are close to the insight that each gratification points to the ultimate one, and that all happiness has some connection with eternal beatitude. Some connection, if only this: that every fulfillment this side of Heaven instantly reveals its inadequacy. It is immediately evident that such satisfactions are not enough; they are not what we have really sought; they cannot really satisfy us at all.

André Gide noted in his *Journals:* "The terrible thing is that we can never make ourselves drunk enough."[5] We may say this of every form of intoxication, not only that of the senses. But for what and to what end is it not "enough"? Why is this insufficiency so terrible? Through all the vulgarization of the concept of happiness a coded but unmistakable message penetrates to us: a reminder of the true and ultimate meaning of happiness. So, too, the phrase "happy ending" is nothing but the old *eudaimonikè teleté* of the Greek mysteries, translated into the jargon of the international motion-picture audience; the original significance is still there, concealed but decipherable, overlaid though it is by what is false and tawdry. It is never utterly lost; it can always break through unexpectedly, like a walled-in fire.

One might take the statement that contemplation is man's ultimate happiness and say to oneself: "Very well, obviously this refers to the 'happiness of the philosopher.' Undeniably there does exist a happiness of knowledge and insight, just as there is happiness in action and 'happiness of the senses.' Certainly it can also be maintained, with good reason, that the happiness of the perceptive mind surpasses all other forms of happiness in depth and value."

All very well. Yet to interpret the sentence in this way, to put so special a construction on it, is to ignore its real meaning. For it says not a word about any special happiness that pertains only to the "philosopher." The dictum speaks of the happiness of man in general, of the whole, physical, earthly, human man. And contemplation is not held up as one among other modes of happiness, even though an especially lofty one. Rather, what it says is this: however the human craving for happiness may time and again be distracted by a thousand small gratifications, it remains directed unwaveringly toward one ultimate satisfaction which is in truth its aim. "Amid a thousand twigs," says Vergil in Dante's universal poem, "one sweet fruit is sought."[6] The finding of this fruit, the ultimate gratification of human nature, the ultimate satiation of man's deepest thirst, takes place in contemplation!

Certainly this exegesis has stripped our dictum of none of its strangeness. Rather the opposite. For how can the most intense craving of our nature be entirely satisfied by an act of the intellect? Would it not be more to the point to speak of love, of becoming one with the Infinite, of drowning ourselves in an ocean of joy? These are precisely the questions we must attempt to answer in the following pages.

II

Man craves by nature happiness and bliss. This statement, which is meant to be taken literally, has a more militant character than may be immediately apparent. It is far from the same as saying that nothing is more natural than that men should want to be happy. No: we want happiness *by nature*. *We* means: all beings endowed with reason. Only a person is capable of being happy—and unhappy—at all. It would be a mis-term to call an animal happy.[1] This, then, must be kept in mind: the directing of the will, through which man strives for his own happiness, has the quality of a natural process.

Thomas Aquinas, it seems, was moved to seek ever-new formulations in which to express this idea. "Man desires happiness naturally and by necessity."[2] "By nature the creature endowed with reason wishes to be happy."[3] "To desire to be happy is not a matter of free choice."[4] "The desire for the ultimate goal is not among the things under our control."[5] This last sentence introduces a new concept: the thought that "happiness" is the name for the ultimate goal of human life.[6] Whether or not we desire the ultimate goal, Thomas says, cannot possibly be made the subject of discussion and decision; it has already been decided over our heads. Before any possibility of our own choice arises, we are already irrevocably "on the way." And the destination is called happiness. Happiness can virtually be defined as the epitome of those things which "the will is incapable of not willing."[7]

What, then, is being asserted here? If "by nature" means that there is no possibility of choice; if the naturalness of a process consists in its being held to a single direction and form; if the *determinatio ad unum*[8] is the distinguishing characteristic, then what is being asserted in the most explicit manner is: that man, as a reasoning being, desires his own happiness just as the falling stone "seeks" the depths, as the flower turns to the light and the beast hunts its prey.

But does this not mean that in the center of the mind's domain something altogether irrational is taking place? Is it not a contradiction to speak of man's "by nature willing" something? To will must either be what it has always been thought to be, an act of the mind, and therefore not an aspect of nature; or else it is a natural process, and therefore not an act of the mind.

This difficulty is indeed insoluble so long as we

insist that "nature" and "mind" are mutually exclusive concepts. This, however, the great teachers of the Occident have always contested. They have steadily maintained there is one being which is in a precise sense both mind and nature simultaneously. This being is the created human soul. "By nature" means: by virtue of creation.[9] All being and activity is "by nature" which—from within the central core of things—flows directly out of the primal impulse of the act of creation, by which creatures have become what they are. Part of the definition of the created soul, therefore, is that it has received its essence—and along with that its assignment in life—from elsewhere, *ab alio*, from the shaping and life-giving act of creation. It necessarily follows that in the center of the created soul something happens which is its own act, and therefore an act of mind, but simultaneously a natural process "by virtue of creation."[10] The desire for happiness is of precisely this character; it is "willing by nature," which is to say an act of the mind and a natural process at one and the same time.

As we might expect, here opinions differ. For at this point the question inevitably arises whether man understands himself as a creature or not. Yes or no? Those who answer "no" cannot accept the idea of a desire for happiness inherent in man's composition; that idea appears to them a slur upon man's autonomous spirit. Only if we understand man as a created being to the very depths of his spiritual existence can we meaningfully conceive that the will has not the power to not want happiness.

But then what about freedom of the will, if it is in this respect unfree? There are two points to be made. First, the natural desire for happiness springs from the innermost core of man's being[11]; it concerns man's very own will, unrestricted by any external coercion. And therefore it is free. Secondly, this desire points, right through the human heart, back to an ultimate origin which is not human. Man has not by his own resolve set in motion his desire for happiness; it has not been given to him to desire otherwise. And therefore "freedom" is not the right term here. There is no avoiding the troublesomeness of such complexity; the subject cannot be reduced to a simple formula. The concept of freedom, too, reveals a new aspect when we think of it in connection with man's createdness. Even St. Thomas, great clarifier as he was, could only state the matter thus: "The will strives in freedom for felicity, although it strives for it by necessity."[12]

In desiring happiness, then, we are obeying a gravitational impulse whose axis is entirely within our own hearts. But we have no power over it—because we ourselves are this gravitational impulse. When we desire to be happy, something blind and obscure takes place within the mind, which nevertheless does not cease to be a light and seeing eye. Something happens "behind" which we cannot penetrate, whose reason we do not see, and for which we can name no reason. Why do you want to be happy? We do not ask—because no one knows the answer.

Plato says precisely this in the *Symposium*,[13] in the dialogue between Diotima and Socrates: " 'If he who loves loves the good, what is it then that he loves?' 'The possession of the good,' I said. 'And what does he gain who possesses the good?' 'Happiness,' I replied; 'there is less difficulty in answering that question.' 'Yes,' she said, 'the happy are made happy by the acquisition of good things. Nor is there any need to ask why a man desires happiness; the answer is already final.' "

From the vantage point of this insight it appears most odd to say that man is a "needy being" only "in so far as he belongs to the sensual world."[14] Rather, the thirst of man's spirit for happiness reveals the inadequacy and neediness of man as creature far more plainly and poignantly than the needs of the body—which by comparison resemble the easily met wishes of a child. To be sure, this idea is difficult to reconcile with the doctrine that the dignity of man consists in his refusing to obey any law but one he imposes upon himself[15] and which, quite consistently, sees the desire for happiness as "the direct antithesis of the principle of morality."[16]

The concept of a nature-dictated desire for happiness has still another implication.

"By felicity," Thomas wrote as a young man,[17] "everyone understands a state perfect to the highest degree; but in what this state consists is hidden"— *occulta quantum ad substantiam*. Once more we are struck by his closeness to Plato: The soul of the lover craves, as we read in the *Symposium*,[18] "something else" besides pleasure—"which she evidently desires and cannot tell, and of which she has only a dark and doubtful presentiment."

Because our turning toward happiness is a blind seeking, we are, whenever happiness comes our way, the recipients of something unforeseen, something unforeseeable, and therefore not subject to planning and intention. Happiness is essentially a gift; we are not the forgers of our own felicity. (That is even true of good *fortune*—which certainly does not necessarily involve happiness.) Surely the "attainment of a created good" can frequently be brought about by purposeful activity. By cleverness, energy, and diligence one can acquire a good many of the goods which are generally considered adjuncts of the happy life: food and drink, house, garden, books, a rich and beautiful wife (perhaps). But we cannot make all these acquisitions, or even a single one of them, quench that thirst so mysterious to ourselves for what we call "happiness," "reflected beatitude." No one can obtain felicity by pursuit. This explains why one of the elements of being happy is the feeling that a debt of gratitude is owed, a debt impossible to pay. Now, we do not owe gratitude to ourselves. To be conscious of gratitude is to acknowledge a gift.

This, too, then seems to reside in the dictum that we desire happiness by nature: that we cannot make ourselves happy.[19]

The contrary attitude of stoic self-sufficiency may still command our respect and admiration. There is "greatness" in the unyielding resolve to desire only what is entirely ours, what we ourselves have acquired. As Seneca has expressed it: "The man is happy, we say, who knows no good that would be greater than that which he can give to himself."[20] Nevertheless, the keener eye will not fail to observe behind all the brave banners and heroic symbols the profound nonhumanity, the submerged anxiety, the senile rigidity, the tension of such an attitude. And our admiration becomes tinged with consternation and horror as it becomes apparent to us how closely such self-sufficiency verges on despair. "Suppose he lacks his miserable bread? What does that matter to one who lacks not the knowledge of how to go to his death?" This sentence, too, may be found in Seneca's book on the happy life.[21]

Finally, when it is said that man by nature seeks happiness, the statement obviously implies that by nature he does not already possess it. "In the present life perfect happiness cannot be."[22] Man is not happy by virtue of his being. Rather, his whole existence is determined precisely by the nonpossession of ultimate gratification. That, after all, is the significance of the concept of *status viatoris*. To exist as man means to be "on the way" and therefore to be nonhappy.[23]

Naturally, man does not cease to be man when he reaches the goal of his way. But it remains true that the concept of an Eternal Life, which simultaneously is Eternal Rest, cannot be grasped by our limited minds. Constituted as we are, we are incapable of even conceiving as an embodied reality the perfectly happy man, that is to say, one whose thirst has been finally quenched and who nevertheless continues to be a living human being.

There is only one Being that is happy by His mere existence. "To God alone may perfect beatitude be attributed, by virtue of His nature."[24]

III

The religious sense of our time allows small place, if any, to the thought that perfect happiness is one of the "attributes" of God. We may almost say that this concept is alien to us.

In St. Thomas's *Summa Theologica*,[1] on the other hand, we read that it would be to miss the reality of God not to think of Him as the perfectly happy Being. I must spend a little time over this aspect of Occidental theology's concept of God.

First of all: the meaning of the statement is not solely that God is happy. Rather, the intention and the words are: "He is His happiness."[2] Indeed, "God and happiness are the same."[3] Any human being who is happy shares in a happiness that is not of himself. For God, however, being and being happy are one and the same; God is happy by virtue of His existence.

This idea immediately gives rise to a disturbing implication. If God's happiness does not rest upon anything's happening, it cannot be diminished or intensified by any events whatsoever in the realm of Creation and in the historical world of man.

That is, in truth, a notion of frightful import. Thomas expressed it in his treatise on the Creation in a sentence of supernal clarity: "The beatitude of God consists not in the action by which He established the Creation, but in the action by which He enjoys Himself, needing not the Creation"—*creaturis non egens.*[4]

Nevertheless, belief that the world itself, its roots and the whole of it, is sound, plumb, and in order, could rest upon no firmer foundation than this doctrine of God's unassailable happiness. If God were not happy, or if His happiness depended upon what happened in the human realm and not upon Himself alone, if His happiness were not beyond any conceivable possibility of disturbance; if there were not, in the Source of reality, this infinitely, inviolably sound Being—we would not be able even to conceive the idea of a possible healing of the empirical wounds of Creation.[5]

From time to time in the history of thought men expressly refuse to name "happiness" as the goal of existence. We must ask ourselves what are the deeper roots of this harsh and distressing position. And we suspect that it is bound up with the idea of God, or more precisely, with inability or refusal to frame the concept of divine beatitude. Always, however, when the success or failure of existence as a whole is under discussion, the question of the solidity of the ultimate ground of being is raised.

This is confirmed from another angle. The mind considering the course of the world, the mind seeking coherency and plunged more and more hopelessly into confusion by the incoherencies of the world, will in the end inevitably be tempted to think (and this temptation comes precisely to the deepest and most consistent thinkers): God is not at one with Himself; God is not happy.

That confidence in the wholeness of being, on the other hand, which finds its ultimate support in the absolute happiness of God, is in no way an invalid simplification of historical reality. Rather, we may say that, far from simplifying things, it reveals them as enormously more complicated and tragic—since the incomprehensibility of evil in the world becomes fully apparent against the background of the indestructible happiness of God. Nevertheless, this belief means that, as Paul Claudel[6] has formulated it, "The terrible words . . . 'In the end truth, perhaps, is sad,' " miss the underlying reality of the world; that, rather, "the great divine joy [is] the only reality."

IV

"To seek happiness is nothing but to seek the satiation of the will"—*ut voluntas satietur*.[1] Thus, the entire energy of human nature is considered a hunger which demands satiation, a thirst that requires quenching. And the quenching of this thirst is happiness.

This metaphor, as telling a one as might be wished, immediately conveys the idea that happiness is being dealt with in a twofold sense. The thirsting man looks toward the glass filled with wine; the hungry man reaches toward a loaf of bread. That is gratification. But we can also say that neither the bread nor the wine is the gratification, but the eating and the drinking of them. Both manners of expression are meaningful and validated by linguistic usage. This is a formal pattern which is frequently encountered. For example, Thomas says: "The goal is spoken of in a dual sense; it can mean the thing we seek to attain, and it can mean its attainment."[2]

The following section, therefore, shall consist of two parts, one dealing with "happiness as drink" and the other with "happiness as drinking."[3] First we must investigate the substance of the drink which is adequate to quench our thirst entirely, to satiate us when we drink of it. The second question is: How may we imagine the drinking of this drink?

If we understand happiness as the quenching of a thirst, we must forthwith recognize that the thirster looks away from himself, that he seeks something else. "That which produces happiness is something outside of the soul."[4] It is inherent in the concepts of hunger and thirst that their gratification is expected from "elsewhere," and that no one can requite himself with himself and by himself alone. If the thirster were himself the drink, or if he possessed it—how could he thirst?

But perhaps exception will be taken to this very thesis: that man is by nature athirst. Once again we must conjure up the figure of the Stoic—a figure whose contemporaneity repeatedly surprises us. "It suffices me to enjoy my own mind"—in an imaginary dialogue[5] Augustine puts these words into the mouth of one of those Stoic sages who according to the account in the New Testament (Acts 17, 18) debated with the Apostle Paul in the Agora of Athens. Opposed to this self-sufficiency is the conviction that man in truth is so constituted that he constantly needs something outside himself; indeed, that he not only needs to receive and to turn to that something perpetually, but that he also shares constantly in it.

Nor can man quench his thirst by his own doing and being right. "Virtue is its own reward"; "the having done it is the recompense for what is done rightly"—this again is the voice of Seneca.[6] Do we not agree? Does not the moral act truly confer a satisfaction which makes for deeper happiness than any gift that one man can transmit to another? No one denies this. But what the Occidental theory of happiness holds is this: that man cannot live by such happiness. The deepest thirst cannot be allayed in this way; the true expectation of the human heart will not accept such a substitute. Wherever such an attitude has been attempted or asserted, it has been artificial and imposed—because it has been something against nature. The "Titan's" arrogance which wants nothing as a gift demands in reality not too much but too little—this is true, surprising though it may at first seem. Such arrogance is too soon contented; it lags behind the true greatness of man.

In his *City of God*[7] Augustine remarks that ancient philosophy offered no less than two hundred and eighty-eight different opinions on what the ultimate happiness of man consists in. After his time, too, as we know, this question was examined —from Boethius to the French moralists—again and again, more or less systematically. Thomas, too, treated it in detail, especially in the two *Summae* and in his *Commentary on Aristotle's Nicomachean Ethics.*[8]

It is no secret that nowadays we cannot muster up much patience or inclination for reading of this sort. After all, we have learned that happiness does not consist in wealth, nor in honors, fame, and so on. A good many comments might be made on this score—for example, that these are probably some of the eternal, fundamental questions of our inner lives. The language in which they are couched changes continually, but they must be faced, and by no means only in the abstract. Nevertheless, I do not intend to burden this little book with all the information on the subject, that, say, Thomas Aquinas might provide. Some of his remarks, however, strike so directly to the heart of our own concern that we must briefly mention them.

For example, there is the concept—one that enters quite unexpectedly here—of "artificial wealth," by which is meant those possessions a person does not immediately need.[9] Artificial wealth, says

Thomas, has the power to engender an infinite craving[10]—and that means: an illusory specter of the desire for happiness.

We might also mention another insight of his, tossed off casually as if it were altogether self-evident. This is his repudiation of the perennial view that existence itself is happiness,[11] that salvation may be equated with physical existence. That view is ultimately the hidden premise of the totalitarian debasement of man to a factor of production, of biologism in every form, of the tendency to make a religion out of psychotherapy. Thomas saw that a being obviously directed toward something else "cannot possibly have as his ultimate goal the preservation of his own existence."[12] In other words, the allaying of the thirst cannot consist simply in the mere continued existence of the thirster.

How surprising, too, is the thought that the happy person cannot be judged and hence also cannot be praised by anyone else. "We do not praise him who has attained the ultimate goal"[13]; he requires "something better than praise."[14] And therefore, says Thomas, happiness cannot consist in "glory," for to have glory means to be praised[15] and judged. To be sure, "glory before God," *gloria* in its full sense, is only another name for beatitude itself. Here too, with a precision we are unaccustomed to, the original meaning is taken literally: man's knowledge, even when it is without error, does not affect the being of what is known; God's knowledge, however, creates being. "We are, in that God sees us," says Augustine.[16] This accounts for the "therefore" which links the following two propositions from the *Summa Theologica:* "The good of man depends upon God's cognition, and *therefore* man's happiness depends upon his glory before God."[17]

And why is power not happiness? "Because power has the quality of beginning, but happiness that of the ultimate end."[18] Not a single word of explanation does Thomas add to this noble sentence. He seems to be saying that power by nature has reference to the future and is prisoned within history. Happiness, on the other hand, even the smallest happiness, is like a step out of Time, and the greatest happiness is sharing in Eternity.

But if all these goods are insufficient to satisfy man's thirst singly, might not all of them together make him happy? Here we must recall Cicero's famous formulation[19]: "They are usually called surpassingly happy [*perbeati*] who, after they have won honor and glory in action, are able to spend their lives in a completely ordered community where they may pursue their work unimperilled and enjoy their leisure with dignity." Would this not be enough? But surely it is a utopian dream! True enough. Yet when we say: No, all that is not enough—we are not saying this because we feel such conditions cannot be realized. Neither do we mean that external possessions such as health, intellectual gifts, honor, and peace are not true goods. Thus even Thomas says: "Anyone who refrained from wine to such an extent that he severely tried nature would in some measure incur guilt."[20] Thomas would therefore say: Truly, those goods are not insignificant; nevertheless, they do not suffice if we consider *the* gratification toward which man's real and deepest thirst is directed. Furthermore, it is not that God has promised and made accessible to man a supernatural happiness which immeasurably and incomprehensibly surpasses all possibilities of gratification in the finite world. Naturally Thomas holds this opinion, or rather, this belief. But as yet we are not formally considering this belief. Here all that we are saying is: Man as he is constituted, endowed as he is with a thirst for happiness, cannot have his thirst quenched in the finite realm; and if he thinks or behaves as if that were possible, he is misunderstanding himself, he is acting contrary to his own nature. The whole world would not suffice this "natural" nature of man. If the whole world were given to him, he would have to say, and would say: It is too little. Too little, that is, to "gratify entirely the power of desire,"[21] or in other words, too little to make him happy.

What, then, is the drink known as happiness which can ultimately suffice this thirst of the whole human being? The long-expected answer is: God. But Thomas does not yet give this answer. And I believe his "postponement" of the answer calls for reflection. It is altogether typical of Thomas, and has to do with his rational sobriety, which at times has been attributed to a lack of spirituality. In reality, this very hesitancy, it seems to me, springs from religious roots. He interposes a concept which we must scrutinize; only then can we appreciate the tremendous import of the answer. Thomas, then, does not say at once: God. He says: *bonum universale.*

This phrase is not easy to translate accurately. "The general good," or "the good in general," would be far too weak, and almost misleading. For Thomas does not mean anything abstract; he means something extremely concrete which is at the same time comprehensive. Perhaps we may translate: "the whole good"—goodness so very good that there is nothing in it which is not good, and nothing outside of it which could be good. Nothing less than this *bonum universale* can quench completely and ultimately man's deepest thirst.[22]

We must observe the uncompromising radicality implicit in this idea. The will craves this *bonum universale*. That is to say: if anywhere in the world a given good exists which it has not yet received, the will desires that good also. We must understand that here Thomas is taking into account the boundlessness of man's craving for happiness, a boundlessness which can be almost terrifying, and which, apparently, only dreams and fairy tales can fulfill. That craving remains in spite of all forms of the "despair of weakness,"[23] that despair which means that we do not want to be ourselves. All purely worldly goals, whether their name be "the classless society" or "prosperity" or "the solitary soul of sylvan glades, who in his integrity is sufficient unto himself," or on the other hand less pretentious programs, such as "muddling through life" or, still more vulgarly, "having a good time because tomorrow we'll all be dead"—all these secularized formulas represent, if they are conceived or sought as ultimate goals, varieties of loss and despair. They all agree on one point: they do not carry their reasoning far enough, to the ultimate conclusion that man's thirst can be fully quenched only by nothing less than "the whole good." This ultimate, however, is named God. Here for the first time Thomas employs this name—after its inevitability has become obvious to all. "The whole good cannot be found anywhere in the realm of created things; it is encountered in God alone."[24]

Once more: we must not imagine that this sentence is a "theological" statement. Rather, Thomas is trying to define what a "finite spirit" is like. For the finite spirit, although it is only a "fragment" of being, by the very fact that it is spirit, is related to the whole of reality. It is required by its nature to deal with everything that is, with the totality of being, of truth, of good. But this means that the finite spirit by virtue of its essence is unquenchable and insatiable—unless it partakes of God.

This is not something to be taken for granted! Quite the contrary: the mysteries inherent in the nature of finite spirit amaze and confound us again and again. How can the Infinite (and the Infinite One!) be the "natural" object of a finite force? Thomas himself, casting an objection into the path of his own thought as is his wont, raises this question: How can man be capable of "grasping a good which exceeds the limits of all creation"?[25] He then replies in this fashion: *Capacitas*, mental grasp, may have two meanings—on the one hand the capacity to receive something from outside into oneself, to embrace it, to take it in and give it shelter within the self. On the other hand, *capacitas* may also mean the power of having something outside as an object. If we understand the capacity of man's mind in the first sense, then it is limited to the sphere of creation; but in the second sense it reaches beyond creation into the infinite.[26] The logic of this is impeccable. But it does not explain anything at all. It only formulates once again the paradoxical state of affairs.

Now, that satiation by the infinite good bears the name happiness or beatitude—and all the other names that language has propounded for the ultimate fulfillment of man: Eternal Life, Eternal Serenity, Eternal Light, Great Banquet, Eternal Glory, Peace, Salvation.

V

Anyone reading nowadays what the ancients wrote on happiness will occasionally sense a peculiar aloofness from the subject, the breath of a disturbing coolness which seems to issue from these texts. If we attempt to get to the bottom of this perplexing sensation, we will soon realize that it cannot be explained solely by the greater objectivity of the Latin language, or the classical modes of presentation. The alien quality is also inherent in the content. In retrospect we may suddenly discover that in those treatises, which aim so hard at systematic completeness, the authors scarcely ever speak of the overwhelming gladness of the heart, nor of the kindling of the mind or the delight of the emotions. But can real happiness be even conceivable without these? Indeed, ought we not say that fundamentally happiness is nothing but gladness, overflowing, infinite joy?

Thomas Aquinas would counter with an unequivocal "no." He would say: Happiness without joy is unthinkable; but joy and happiness are two different things. Evidently the matter is highly

complex. But his statement, which at the outset
seems scarcely intelligible, merits examination.

In the first place, what Thomas says does not
imply contempt for the "affects" or for the element of passion. Such contempt does exist, we
know, and is to be found in the writings of the ancients too—for example, in some of the Stoics.
However, we must remember that the term "the
ancients" has two separate and distinct meanings.
In its most exact sense, it refers not to the writers
of the past but to the witnesses of that great, in-
tegral, all-embracing tradition of wisdom fed by
the Divine Logos which can be found in all ages.[1]
And among these, of course, we do not find contempt for anything that pertains to the stuff of
reality or to human nature. Thus Thomas takes it
completely for granted that no full beatitude can
be conceived without pleasure, gladness, enjoy-
ment, rapture on the part of the physical, spiritual-
sensual being which is man.[2] How could the conception of physical well-being seriously be omitted
by anyone who believes in the resurrection of the
dead?

At this point a difficulty in translation crops up,
one which somewhat hampers our understanding.
Our words "delight" and "delectation" do not precisely correspond to the Latin *delectatio,* which

means simultaneously the spiritual joy of the heart and mind and the pleasure of man's sensual nature. Thomas, however, is referring to both when he says that in happiness are supremely united goodness, beauty, desirability, and *delectabilissimum*, that which confers profoundest pleasure.[3]

Nevertheless, happiness and joy are not the same. For what does the fervent craving for joy mean? It does not mean that we wish at any cost to experience the psychic state of being joyful. We want to have *reason* for joy, for an unceasing joy that fills us utterly, sweeps all before it, exceeds all measure. This reason is, if it exists, anterior to joy, and is in itself something different from joy. Joyousness necessarily implies an "about something"; we cannot rejoice in the absolute; there is no joy for joy's sake. This something, this reason, is our possessing or receiving a thing we desire. "Possession of the good is the cause of rejoicing."[4] This having and partaking of the good is primary; joy is secondary. In the *Summa Theologica* these ideas are expressed in the following manner: "Therefore a person rejoices because he possesses a good appropriate to him—whether in reality, or in hope, or at least in memory. The appropriate good, however, if it is perfect, is precisely the man's happiness. . . . Thus it is evident that not even the joy which follows the

45

possession of the perfect good is the essence of happiness itself."[5]

We have distinguished between the drink and the act of drinking. This image immediately makes plain that the "drink known as happiness," which is something outside of the soul, *aliquid extra animam*, cannot be equated with joy. But it is also true that "happiness as drinking," which like joy is an act of the soul, *aliquid animae*,[6] is also something different from joy. We might pursue the image in the following way: Just as the state of having drunk and the good taste of the drink are two different things, so too happiness and joy are two different things.

Moreover, this idea once again underlines the fact that joy is essentially a consequence, is essentially a response to the attainment of a good; in individual cases it may even be an erroneous response, but it always points back to the original and preceding cause. It is not, then, an illusionary sport of disparate emotions. Implied, too, is a far-reaching concomitant: confidence in the "realness" of life's continuities in general. And bound up with it is the conviction that any attempt to acquire joy "as needed," like a drug, is hopelessly vain.

There is further indication that joy does not occupy the highest rank in the logical series: namely, that there are goods which we desire even though possession of them does not yield joy. These are the goods which we crave by our very nature precisely as we crave happiness; we may also say that they are direct components of the substance of happiness. What goods might these be? Thomas mentions sight, memory, knowledge, being good[7]; he scarcely intends a complete list, although his choices are not accidental. Three of these four ideas refer to awareness of reality: awareness by seeing, knowing, remembering. We want to know the truth at any cost, even if the truth should be frightful. I should add at once, however, that I have not exactly reproduced St. Thomas's thought. He speaks in the subjunctive: we would even desire certain goods if they were not to yield joy, *etiamsi nulla delectatio ex his sequeretur.*[8] For the truth is that knowledge, even of frightful things, satisfies the human heart in such a manner that even here we may speak of joy.

But in that case, too, joy is something additional, something secondary.

Now if some person, not convinced by the previous arguments, should refer to his inner experience and say: But we obviously do not seek joy as a means to something else, but as something ultimate in itself, just as we seek happiness; and if the question, Why do we wish to be happy, is meaningless, than it is equally meaningless, in fact downright ridiculous, to ask: Why do you wish to rejoice? If a person were to speak thus, he would be formulating an objection which Thomas himself raises in almost these very words.[9] He too says it is "ridiculous" to ask the reason for our desire for joy. Here is a conundrum which we must briefly discuss.

Thomas answers it in such a way that at first he seems to admit the validity of the objection: "Joy is sought not on account of something else, but on account of itself. . . ."[10] What, we may ask, then becomes of the thesis that joy is something secondary? But we have not allowed Thomas to finish. "On account of anything else," he goes on to say, can have two meanings. It can refer to the relationship of means and end. And the fact remains that joy is not the means to any end; no one seeks joy in order to attain something else. But the other possible meaning of "on account of" is this: it can refer to the motive and object of willing. And understood in this sense, joy is actually sought "on account of something else," namely, "on account of the good which is its object."[11]

An aside. This last sentence does not imply, it

must be so, but rather: it is so; this is what happens whenever we rejoice. Nor is this meant in any moralistic sense. "Good" does not mean here "the ethical good" which, as Kant would have it, "must be willed for its own sake." Rather, it means every "drink" which quenches any thirst. And in the Latin text the word used for "joy" is always *delectatio*, which, to repeat, embraces both sensual and spiritual gladness.

Because joy is nothing but the *quietatio appetitus in bono*, the appeasement of desire in the good that has been made one's own—therefore this good is always what is primarily sought in joy: *within* joy, not by any means *beyond* joy.

"All beings desire joy in the same manner, as they also desire what is good for them. Nevertheless they desire joy for the sake of the good, and not the converse. . . . Thus it follows that . . . every joy is consequent to a good, and that there exists a joy consequent to that which is in itself the supreme good."[12]

The "supreme good" and its attainment—that is happiness. And joy is: response to happiness.

VI

It is hard to conceive of attaining "the whole good." The difficulty lies in our lack of clarity about the meaning of the word "attain" in this connection. Everyone knows what the process of attaining a tangible thing is. I shake a ripe apple from the tree; I pick it up and put it into my pocket; and finally I eat it. This, then, is the question: What corresponds to this picking up and eating when we are discussing "the whole good," when we are concerned with obtaining it, possessing it, and enjoying it? What is the process of appropriation and "ingestion" in this case? We do not become happy by the mere fact that happiness as a drink, as something outside of the soul, *extra animam*, exists. Rather, there is something we must partake of, receive and make part of us. How can we conceive of this partaking?

Obviously this depends both upon the nature of the drink and the nature of the drinker. This, by the way, is the reason any answer to this question inevitably involves a statement on the essence of God, on human nature, and on the relationship between the Creator and the creature—subjects, in other words, that no one completely understands. (When we remember this from the outset, we realize how little personal opinions count in this matter; rather, the more personal these are, the more wary we should be of them.)

The "whole good" cannot be had, it would seem, without mustering all the strength of our inner life. Even in the sphere of external possessions there are goods which inherently demand, if they are to be truly ours, far more of us than mere acquisition. " 'My garden,' the rich man said; his gardener smiled."[1] How do we possess a work of art? By buying it or receiving it as a gift? At what point do we "get" anything out of it?

It might be said: The process of becoming happy is like being overwhelmed by a tremendous wave. Eckhart seems to mean something of the sort when he speaks of the "naked essence of the soul" which passively experiences happiness without any act of its own[2]—as a liquid pours into an empty vessel. The Eastern branch of Christendom also seems to favor this theory. Nevertheless, we must raise the question of whether it is not, when pursued to its logical conclusion, an idea contrary to the nature of man. We do not even partake of an ordinary glass of wine in this manner; it does not merely flow into us.

Rather, we drink it actively and transform it into our own substance. To be sure, if we make this point we must be prepared for the countering argument: Therein lies the unique property of the divine good, for it is so immeasurable that it cannot be seized and "assimilated" by us. This, too, would explain why we do not take into ourselves the "joy of the Lord," but conversely are destined to "enter into" it (Matt. 25:21).

Here we must take account of one of St. Thomas's conceptual distinctions, which at first seems like unnecessary cavilling. It is the distinction between "uncreated" and "created" happiness (*beatitudo increata—beatitudo creata*).[3] We have here something which, while not at all obvious, is nevertheless fraught with consequences for our whole feeling about life. Namely, this: what does indeed make us happy is the infinite and uncreated richness of God; but participation in this, happiness itself, is entirely a "creatural" reality governed from within by our humanity; it is *not* something that descends overwhelmingly upon us from outside. That is, it is not only something that happens to us; we ourselves are intensely active participants in our own happiness.

Beatitude—Thomas is saying—cannot possibly be conceived as a merely objective condition of sheer existence. It is not a mere quality, not pure passivity, not simply a feeling.[4] It is something that takes place in the alert core of the mind.

We have posed the question: in what way may we conceive appropriation and consuming if the matter in question is not an apple, but "the whole good." A first element of the answer, laid down by Occidental tradition, would be: the attainment of this good which we call happiness must take place by action. Happiness is an act and an activity of the soul.[5]

But has it not been said that happiness is always a gift? If this is true, then how can it simultaneously be our own action? To this question a Spanish commentator on the *Summa Theologica* four hundred years ago gave an answer which is as perspicacious as it is simple: If sight were given to a blind man, he would nevertheless see with his own sense of sight.[6] We need not add a word to this reply.

The full force of this idea of happiness as action emerges still more clearly when we see that it is linked in a cohesive logical structure with several of the basic tenets of Occidental teachings on man and reality in general. These are, above all, the following three propositions. First: *Happiness means perfection.* Essential to the concept of happiness is

53

that there is "nothing left to wish for," that the happy person has attained the ultimate goal. "In perfect felicity the whole man is perfected."[7] Second: *Perfection means full realization.*[8] Man attains perfection in so far as the incomplete draft which he is initially is realized, attains to fullest reality. If happiness is equivalent to perfection, then "Felicity must consist in man's attainment of the uttermost degree of being real."[9] Third: *Realization is achieved by action.* This does not mean here that only fussing and straining will yield results. The meaning is rather: "Action is the ultimate realization of the person who acts."[10] That is to say, only by acting does man achieve the fullness of his reality. Naturally, he is already real in the sense that he exists before he acts; without existence he could not very well act. That is taken for granted. But there is a mode of achieving reality which goes beyond the mere fact of existing, in which living beings attain to a more intense and "realer" realness—by acting.[11] Happiness, then, as drinking of the drink, must be thought of as a form of acting which opens all the potentialities of man to fullest realization.

This, says Thomas, is also the meaning of the phrase dear to the Scriptures when referring to beatitude: Eternal Life. The term does not mean simply living without end, but the supreme intensification of the state of being alive in a perfect "living-doing"[12] (whereas the conversion of action to its opposite signifies a diminution of life, and is therefore aptly called *passio* in both senses, that of passivity and that of suffering, whose final and ultimate form is death).[13]

We have now reached the point where we may adequately frame the question whose answer we anticipated at the outset. All that we have said hitherto has been an attempt to show how to formulate most precisely that question. We can now state it thus: If "the whole good" alone will ultimately quench the thirst of our natures, and if we can obtain this whole good only by receiving it *actively*; if, in short, happiness consists in action—what kind of action must that be?

First of all, it is not action directed outward toward the gaining of some success in the external world, although to the average mind, limited by an activistic habit of thought, this alone is usually considered activity. Rather, what is meant is an activity which remains within the acting person himself.[14] For acting does not consist only in building, establishing, producing, struggling, killing. Cognition, for example, is true activity. That is to say, it is a realization of the potentialities inherent in the living cell. Nor does only activity directed toward the external world produce results. Activity which remains within the acting self also yields results, although these do not show outwardly. They are a fruit which grows within—for example, the *verbum cordis*,[15] the "heart's word," the still unvoiced fruit of insight.

Here it may be objected that man obviously feels himself happiest when he is able to work in a creatively active fashion in the world, following out his own impulses and plans. Is not the man who labors constructively, the plowman, the gardener, and above all the creative artist, considered the prototype of the happy man, in spite of all the sweat of toil or the pangs of creation—considered so because it is granted to him to bring into the world out of his own body and mind a whole *poiema*, an objective product? To this we may reply that when we distinguish between activity that remains within and activity that reaches out we do mean that the one excludes the other. For activity that reaches out into the world certainly does not affect only the field, the rose bed or the block of marble; it also affects the actor himself. Along with the doing of any work there is an effect which does emerge, but which remains hidden within the doer himself, perhaps chiefly as a fruit of insight, as a *verbum cordis*. Perhaps this fruit can grow only in the course of a man's dealing with the pliable or resistant matter of a garden, or potter's clay, or marble; perhaps this is the only way in which it can grow. And may it not be that in this *processio ad intra*,[16] in this inward fructification, lies the truly beatifying element which we rightly ascribe to all creative activity?

To repeat: the activity in which we receive the drink which is happiness is by its nature an activity whose effects work inward. This cannot be otherwise, for only in such activity does the acting person actualize himself. Action which reaches outward perfects the work rather than the person who acts. Under those circumstances what happens is that the perfection of the work "does not . . . include the creator; he is condemned to return to his lesser ego."[17]

VII

"The essence of happiness consists in an act of the intellect."[1]

Abruptly the gauntlet is cast down. Thomas purports to be giving a precisely co-ordinate reply to the posed question. The challenging nature of his statement is rather stressed than mitigated by the blandness of the dictum. And if criticism and objections spring to mind as soon as we reflect upon the sentence, nothing is more natural. For this is no offhand remark.

What is implicit in this sentence? This is implicit: the fulfillment of existence takes place in the manner in which we become aware of reality; the whole energy of our being is ultimately directed toward attainment of insight. The perfectly happy person, the one whose thirst has been finally quenched, who has attained beatitude—this person is one who sees. The happiness, the quenching, the perfection, consists in this seeing.

Although it is true that all this is primarily said in reference to "eternal bliss" (primarily but not exclusively; we shall have more to say about that in a moment)—the subject under discussion is in any case the ultimate satiation of our own hunger, although the manner in which this is concretely to take place may remain altogether obscure. To say that this satiation will be accomplished by seeing is accordingly to say: Man, physical, historical, "earthly" man, has a basic craving to see; strictly speaking, he craves nothing else; his make-up is such that he lives most purely as a see-er: in contemplation.

It is obvious that these statements strike directly at the foundation of existence. They are not meant to apply only to a particular type of man, say to the scientifically or philosophically minded man, to *homo theoreticus*. Not at all; they apply to *homo sapiens* in general. And if they are true, they mean to the average man of our times no less than this: that he must "change his life." But are they really true? Does not man's perfection consist rather in love, and thus in an inclination of the will? Who, after all, is happier than the lover? Is not love the fashion in which we possess what is "good" for us? And would it not be—as Duns Scotus was fond of saying[2]—a *perversus ordo*, an overturning of the order of things, if a person wished to love in order to attain insight?

These are propositions which, it would seem, no one can seriously contest. Thomas, too, recognizes their cogency, and he has formulated his own thesis expressly with a view to this counterposition. Or rather, he himself develops the opposing argument, and even as he thus acknowledges it, he appropriates it as an enrichment to his own thought. (Thus has true superiority of the intellect ever revealed itself.) For all that, he still means his dictum concerning the essence of happiness to be taken as it stands. So categorical is he about it that his discussion tends to increase our doubts; we feel pretty sure that he has gone too far, has raised to an absolute whole what is only a partial aspect of the matter—and so on. If, for example, someone should say (as did Hugh of St. Victor[3]): "To know truth and love the good—in this happiness consists"—we might think that no one could disagree, that here was an unassailable truth which reconciles contradictions. But Thomas is this no one; he does disagree. The premise is acceptable, he would say, only if the words are taken in an extended sense; taken exactly, the premise is false. "For if that which essentially comprises happiness is meant, then I say: it cannot possibly consist in an act of the will"[4]; according to Thomas, happiness consists in cognitive activity and nothing else.

Thomas formulated this idea many times, and frequently with an emphasis that is unusual for him.[5] Yet the whole insight would be lost on us if we took it as merely a pet notion of the author's, one of the special features of his theory. (For in that case, would it interest anyone but the learned specialist?) Thomas was concerned with articulating a precept hidden within the great tradition and always threatened by oblivion; only against the background of this precept does the relative acceptability of personal opinions emerge. What is under discussion here is nothing less than the inner structure of human nature, indeed of the spirit in general and of reality as a whole. That is, nothing less is under discussion than the ultimate question which has always troubled human reason, in its search for wisdom, in its *philo-sophia*.

But what, in precise terms, is Thomas asserting when he says that happiness takes the form of cognition? That is made manifest by a single sentence in which he answers his own objections. He refers to a sentence of Augustine's from the latter's book on the trinitarian God, a sentence of that striking simplicity which, it would seem, only the greatest thinkers can inscribe: *Beatus est, qui habet omnia quae vult.*[6] "Surpassingly happy is he who has everything he wants." From this it would seem,

Thomas points out, that it is impossible to speak of happiness without speaking of the will.[7] Impossible to answer this objection without speaking of the crux of the matter! How does Thomas deal with the dichotomy? At first he expressly accepts the Augustinian dictum, although he recasts it somewhat: "He who has everything he wants is happy in that he has what he wants."[8] But there then follows, in a terse subsidiary clause, the actual retort; so quietly is it put that perhaps even the adversary will at first fail to notice how completely he has been defeated. The argument is as surprising as it is deadly: "He is happy in that he has what he wants—*which having, however, takes place by something other than an act of will.*"[9] Happiness does consist in having everything that the will can possibly will—Thomas acquiesces to this proposition. It consists in our obtaining as a possession "the whole good." *But*—this having, possessing, obtaining, is something different from willing! The question thereby raised can be formulated as follows: What is having the *bonum universale* toward which our nature strives with all its indwelling energy? How does this having take place, and what is it like, how does it happen? This question is, as we can easily see, identical with the other one which we posed early: How does happiness (as drinking) take place? And to this Thomas replies: The having takes place as cognition; cognition *is* having. In other words: "The essence of happiness consists in an act of the intellect."

At this point we may again lean upon the Spanish Scholastic whose precision of language has already aided us in our task. "The happy life [we read in his commentary on the *Summa Theologica*[10]] does not mean loving what we possess, but possessing what we love." Possession of the beloved, St. Thomas holds, takes place in an act of cognition, in seeing, in intuition, in contemplation.

Thomas is not alone in saying this. The same point is made by Augustine also, although in this matter he is considered to be the counterpoise to Thomas,[11] and although all voluntarists are in the habit of turning to him as their great ancestor—in so far as they are concerned at all with finding within Christian tradition legitimation for their ideas.

Four propositions from Augustine's works may be quoted here; many more in a similar vein might be cited. "Having is nothing but cognition."[12] "What else does being happy mean, if not this: knowingly to possess something eternal?"[13] "No matter how much you labor, you labor to this end:

that you may see."[14] "Our whole reward is seeing," *tota merces nostra visio est.*[15]

Such consonance, surprising to those who take the usual view of Thomas and Augustine, illuminates the extent to which this concept of the nature of knowing is the common property of the Occidental mind.

The ancients conceived the whole energy of human nature as a hunger. Hunger for what? For being, for undiminished actuality, for complete realization—which is not attainable in the subject's isolated existence, for it can be secured only by taking into the self the universal reality. Hunger is directed toward the real universe, and the universe in its literal sense, toward the whole of being, toward everything that exists. We have all become accustomed to consider this proposition from an "ideal" point of view, to take the statement too figuratively and "spiritually," and thus to falsify or simply obliterate its literal, specific meaning. To be sure, a principle frequently lurks behind such idealization: namely, the desire not to admit that man as a spiritual being can be "needy" at all. In point of fact the word "hunger" should be understood in its most drastic and literal sense. In so far as he exists spiritually, man desires satiation by reality; he 'wants to "have" reality; he hungers for "the whole," longs to be filled to repletion. So furious is this hunger that it would have to be called desperate if there were no hope of satiation.

Old metaphysics, it has been said, was motivated chiefly by this one question: How is reality to be attained; how are we to obtain and receive it; how is it to be grasped, appropriated, incorporated, possessed as a property of ourselves? This is the problem of a *conquête de l'être*, of the conquest of actuality.[16] And the answer is: cognition, spiritual insight. For Thomas as well as for Augustine, cognition is essentially seizure of the world and grasping of reality.[17] To know is by the nature of knowing to have; there is no form of having in which the object is more intensely grasped. In Thomas we more than once[18] find the proposition that knowing is "the highest mode of having." But this, we make haste to add, is not because that mode of having is the "most spiritual"—this would once again be an "idealizing" misconstruction, into which we seem almost necessarily to fall. Rather, knowing is the highest mode of having because in the world there is no other form so thoroughgoing. Knowing is not only appropriation which results in "property" and "proprietorship." It is assimilation in the quite exact sense that the objective world, in so far as it is known, is incorporated into the very being of the knower. This, indeed, distinguishes cognitive from noncognitive beings: the latter have nothing outside themselves, whereas the knower obtains a share in alien beings in that he knows them, that is to say, in that he takes them into himself and, as Thomas puts it, possesses the "form" of these alien beings.[19] Material things have closed boundaries; they are not accessible, cannot be penetrated, by things outside themselves. But one's existence as a spiritual being involves being and remaining oneself *and* at the same time admitting and transforming into oneself the reality of the world. No other material thing can be present in the space occupied by a house, a tree, or a fountain pen. But where there is mind, the totality of things has room; it is "possible that in a single being the comprehensiveness of the whole universe may dwell."[20] This principle is expressed in that great dictum of Aristotle which has become a truism for the Occident: "The soul is at bottom all that is," *anima est quodammodo omnia.*[21]

To sum up once more: Happiness is attained in an act of cognition because there is no other perfect way in which we can truly obtain "the whole good," and all reality in general.

Having clarified these matters, we see how dubious is the habit of opposing "cognition" to "life" —as though cognition were anything but life, as though it were a mere side issue, at best a kind of musical accompaniment but possibly also an obstacle to "actual" life; as though cognition were not itself "the most perfect thing in life," *perfectissimum quod est in vita*[22]; as though it were not that only in cognition, only in alert grasping and comprehending, do we truly take possession of our real wealth.

Having pondered this last thought for a while, it may well happen that, innocently rereading, a sentence like the following strikes like a flash of lightning into our souls: "Eternal life is knowing Thee. . . ." (John 17:3).

VIII

But is not all this in the end "intellectualism," an overvaluing of the part that cognition plays in the whole of existence? Has not the importance of the will and of love been suppressed or misinterpreted? To answer these questions we must "grasp the objects purely," as Goethe put it, and think the arguments through in logical order.

The kernel of willing and loving is affirmation. And there are, Thomas says,[1] fundamentally only two ways in which this affirmation is expressed: in yearning and in joy. Yearning is desire, craving, striving for, seeking, *motus ad finem*—such is the expression of love before the beloved object has become a possession. Joy is rapture, delight, bliss, *fruitio, delectatio*—such is the expression of love which has already obtained the beloved object. Yet obviously this obtaining does not take place in either manner, neither in desiring nor in joy. How can this be denied? We do not desire the desiring. What is ultimately sought by the will cannot itself be an act of will[2]—because all motion seeks rest[3] (and rest is not in willing but in knowing[4]). Always and necessarily, that which is sought and loved becomes present to the will and is obtained by the will through something other than an act of will and of love—so we read in the *Summa Theologica*.[5] This "other," however—we already know the answer—this other is cognition.

To be sure, cognition itself has many modes and degrees. It is clear that we do not obtain reality, do not partake of it, merely by awareness, simply by "knowing about something"; we do not even obtain it by logically arriving at a conclusion. Reality is the prize solely of the highest form of cognition, and that is: seeing, intuition, contemplation. We shall have more to say of this later. But in any case, seeing too is "an act of the intellect." And so it remains unshakably valid that possession of what we love takes place for us through cognition.

It would seem that language has basically only one word to describe what actually happens when we "realize" the presence of another person. That word is "seeing." We have him before our eyes, we see him. All other words are either spatial metaphors (nearness, closeness) or derive from the sense of touch (tangibility, being at hand, being in contact). That is to say, they refer to externalities. A recent account of life in prisoner-of-war camps sets down a conversation between two prisoners lying on their cots who ask one another and themselves what it really is that makes men happy. Their answer is: Being happy is equivalent to being together with those we love.[6] There is no doubt that for these men "being together" could mean only one thing: to *see* their loved ones again.

We may also recall here the Biblical phraseology in which the union of man and woman is referred to as a mutual "knowing."[7] This use of the word is anything but a euphemism. Quite the contrary. The term expresses with matchless precision the exact truth of the matter—as soon as we go back to the original meaning of the Hebrew word. That meaning was: immediate togetherness, intimate presence.[8] (Let us consider for a moment what this implies. In seeking a basis for our characterizing the fact of "presence" by the term "knowing" we suddenly discover that knowing originally derives from a word meaning presence. In the realm of primal words we are always on the verge of tautology.)

All this casts further light on the subject of happiness, especially that striking insight about "being together with those we love." It is not the mere seeing (having, possessing, partaking of) in itself that makes one happy. Happy is he who sees *what he loves*. It is only the presence of the thing or person loved that makes for happiness. That is, without love there is no happiness; if there were no spark of assent and affirmation, there could not even be the possibility of happiness—neither in the mode of seeing nor in any other way. Love is the indispensable premise of happiness. (However, it must also be said that if one does not love one cannot be unhappy. For the essence of unhappiness is the failure to possess what one loves. Even the sorrow of the damned is the sorrow of separation from that which they still steadily love.) Love, then, is necessary for happiness; but it is not enough. Only the presence of what is loved makes us happy, and that presence is actualized by the power of cognition.

It may very well be, however, that the power of seeing itself is only stirred to full realization by love. "Where love is, there is the eye," *ubi amor, ibi oculus*. (One would guess this to be a phrase of Augustine's. But in fact it comes from the commentary on the *Sentences* written by Thomas Aquinas as a young man.[9]) The meaning is that there are things which the lover alone observes; but above all, that the lover partakes of goods which are withheld from all others—which is to say that higher potentialities for happiness are open to him than to anyone else. Nevertheless, no matter what may be observable to his eye by virtue of love, the activity of the eye is still seeing and not loving.

At this point the outlines of the concept of "contemplation" come into view somewhat more distinctly. Actually, contemplation is not simply one possible form among others of the act of knowing. Its special character does not flow from its being a particular aspect of the process of knowing. What distinguishes—in both senses of that word— contemplation is rather this: it is a knowing which is inspired by love. "Without love there would be no contemplation."[10]

Contemplation is a loving attainment of awareness. It is intuition of the beloved object.

IX

The Latin words *contemplatio, contemplari,* correspond to the Greek words *theoria, theorein.*[1] Cicero, Seneca, and undoubtedly many other less famous writers established the Latin words as coordinate with the earlier coined Greek words in the course of those comprehensive labors of translation which characterized the early history of the Latin West.

Theoria has to do with the purely receptive approach to reality, one altogether independent of all practical aims in active life. We may call this approach "disinterested," in that it is altogether divorced from utilitarian ends. In all other respects, however, *theoria* emphatically involves interest, participation, attention, purposiveness. *Theoria* and *contemplatio* devote their full energy to revealing, clarifying, and making manifest the reality which has been sighted; they aim at truth and nothing else. This is the first element of the concept of contemplation: silent perception of reality.

A second is the following: Contemplation is a form of knowing arrived at not by thinking but by seeing, intuition. It is not co-ordinate with the *ratio*, with the power of discursive thinking, but with the *intellectus*, with the capacity for "simple intuition."[2] Intuition is without doubt the perfect form of knowing. For intuition is knowledge of what is actually present; the parallel to seeing with the senses is exact. Thinking, on the other hand, is knowledge of what is absent, or may be merely the effort to achieve such knowledge; the subject matter of thinking is investigated by way of something else which is directly present to the mind, but the subject matter is not seen as it is in itself. The validity of thinking, Thomas says, rests upon what we perceive by direct intuition; but the necessity for thinking is due to a failure of intuition.[3] Reason is an imperfect form of *intellectus*.[4] Contemplation, then, is intuition; that is to say, it is a type of knowing which does not merely move toward its object, but already rests in it. The object is present—as a face or a landscape is present to the eye when the gaze "rests upon it." In intuition there is no "future tension,"[5] no desire directed toward the future, which desire corresponds with the nature of thinking. The person who knows by intuition has already found what the thinker is seeking; what he knows is present "before his eyes." This presence, however, this spatial "thereness," may at any moment be converted into temporal "presence," which is a tense-form of Eternity.[6]

A third element remains to be mentioned. Traditionally, contemplation has been characterized as a knowing accompanied by amazement.[7] In contemplation a *mirandum* is seen, that is to say, a reality which evokes amazement because it exceeds our comprehension even though we see it, and have a direct intuition of it. Amazement is possible only for one who does not yet see the whole; God cannot be amazed.[8] One of the characteristics of earthly contemplation is this accompaniment of unease in the face of the unattainable. Quite aside from the distraction caused by the requirements of physical life —a distraction which is both inescapable and wholesome—there inevitably intrudes into the midst of the peace of contemplation the soundless call to another, infinitely profounder, incomprehensible, "eternal" peace. This is "the call of perfection to the imperfect, which call we name love."[9] It inclines toward that other love which we have named as the inspiring source of contemplation.

X

"Earthly contemplation"—these are the words we have used. They delimit fairly precisely the matter we are really concerned with. However, the two words represent a union of virtual incompatibles. For contemplation means our partaking of "the whole good" in the form of intuitive having; and we cannot speak of "intuiting" in the air; if we speak of "drinking" we cannot be silent about the "beverage." How, then, can earthly contemplation be possible, since "seeing God" is denied to man on earth? Do we in the end have to say that the dictum about contemplation's being the ultimate of human happiness refers simply to *eternal* bliss and to nothing else? Now the distinguishing trait of the Occidental doctrine of the "contemplative life" is a persistent negative answer to this question. We must try to understand the why and wherefore of this position.

That ultimate satiation with the drink known as "happiness" takes place the other side of death, when God is seen "face to face"—this is an inviolable truth to which all traditions accede. Thomas says that this seeing, to which, incidentally, he also applies the name "contemplation," constitutes the eternal beatitude not only of men and angels but of God Himself—and adds that this is the opinion of the "philosophers" as well as the "saints."[1]

Nevertheless, there lies within this eschatological assertion in regard to the ultimate perfection of things an anthropological statement concerning the nature of man and his historical existence. It is this statement we are primarily concerned with, although we are well aware that without the other it could never have been thought out and developed so clearly, or even preserved at all.

If the ultimate fulfillment in the hereafter is to be called "seeing" (*visio*), this is tantamount to saying that man here on earth is at bottom a being who craves to see. This we have already discussed. Within the concept of earthly contemplation, however, lies a more exact assertion which goes beyond this. One element of this concept has already been stated. Such contemplation, we have said, must be imagined as a focusing of the inner gaze, undistracted by anything from outside, but troubled from within by the challenge to achieve a profounder but unattainable peace. It must be imagined as a satisfaction which desires nothing "else" and yet is not satisfied with itself because in its uttermost depths, yet insuperably remote, a still more complete satisfaction is sensed.

Furthermore, this earthly existence can offer us an awareness of "the whole," of the very essence of all that is "good" for us—a knowing of God, in other words, which is the result neither of logical reasoning nor of simple faith. "Human happiness does not consist in the knowledge of God, which is to be had by logical demonstration."[2] But faith, too, precisely because it is by definition nonseeing, "rather kindles the longing than gratifies it."[3] The knowledge brought us by faith is knowledge of what is absent.[4] Contemplation, however, including earthly contemplation, is able to quench man's thirst more than anything else because it affords a direct perception of the presence of God; contemplation is the form in which we partake of the uttermost degree of happiness which this physical, historical existence of ours is capable of holding. "Imperfect beatitude, such as can be had here, consists primarily and principally in contemplation,"[5] that is, in earthly contemplation. And: "As far as contemplation extends, so far does happiness extend."[6]

Inherent in this idea, as premises or as corollaries, are several ideas which are not immediately evident. One corollary is that insightful knowledge, spiritual vision, "intellectual intuition," is possible for man here on earth; that man's method of grasping reality is not exclusively thinking, "mental labor," what Hegel called "discursive" effort. The repose of "simple intuition" does exist. As we know, this is by no means an incontrovertible assumption. But to contest it is also to dismiss the idea of earthly contemplation. We must also point out that such denial is fraught with consequences extending into the world of contemporary politics. For example, the inhumanity of totalitarian labor is based, among other things, upon the fact that man is considered as a "worker" even in his intellectual life; he is permitted spare time, but no true repose.[7]

There is still another premise: namely, that not only the *act* of *visio* in the hereafter has its counterpart in this world, a preliminary form, an inchoate foreshadowing; but that, moreover, we must in some manner be able to partake of the *object* of this act, that drink called happiness. We do so in earthly contemplation, no matter what the manner of the drinking may be. This means: God is present in the world; He can appear "before the eyes" of one whose gaze is directed toward the depths of things. A corollary, therefore, is that reality is a creation, and that consequently God is not "outside of the world," not a *Deus extramundanus*, but the acting basis of everything that exists. The Christian, of course, would be able to speak of a special manner of "intuiting" God in the midst of the historical world. For him earthly contemplation means above all: that back of immediate phenomena, and within them, the Face of the incarnate Divine Logos is visible.

So far, however, we have said nothing about the concrete form in which earthly contemplation is actualized.

For a moment we might be tempted to distinguish among several basic forms: religious contemplation, poetic, philosophical, and so on. But it soon becomes evident that such categorization does not tell us very much. The common element proves to be more crucial than the dissimilarities; and we may well ask whether any of the dissimilarities are essential. Above all, it is meaningless to distinguish between religious and nonreligious contemplation. That can be fairly convincingly demonstrated.

We have said that loving knowledge, seeing the beloved object, is the essence of contemplation. This, naturally, is a simplification which might be misunderstood. To be sure, wherever "seeing the beloved object" occurs, there is appeasement and happiness. But this kind of seeing is not necessarily in itself contemplation. Something else is needed. Only when love is directed toward the infinite divine appeasement which courses through all reality from the ultimate ground of reality; and when this beloved object shows itself to the soul's gaze in a wholly immediate, effortless, utterly tranquil (yet inwardly troubled) self-revelation, even though for no longer than the duration of a lightning flash—only then do we have contemplation in the full meaning of the word. This might even serve as a definition. And if we agree we cannot at the same time admit that there are nonreligious forms of contemplation.

The common element in all the special forms of contemplation is the loving, yearning, affirming bent toward that happiness which is the same as God Himself, and which is the aim and purpose of all that happens in the world.[8] The common element is an approach whose impetus bursts forth from the core of man's being, feeds on the energy of man's whole nature, and carries all the powers of that nature along in its dynamic movement. Within that common element the intrinsic force of the craving for happiness is united with the data of all the senses, with the play of the imagination, with the insights of reason, and with faith and the supernatural New Life—both these last goods granted as free gifts. Without this love directed toward this object, there is no true contemplation. Love alone makes it possible for contemplation to satiate the human heart with the experience of supreme happiness.

This, then, is the common element in all contemplation which rises above all differences and floods all distinguishing marks. In contemplation, the multiple forces of human nature are always called upon, always at play. Who would wish to term "purely religious" the contemplation which underlies St. Francis of Assisi's *Song to the Sun*, or the poems of St. John of the Cross? Is it not simultaneously poetic and philosophic as well? Nevertheless, it is true that such contemplation obviously has been kindled by meditation on the divine mysteries and by prayer. Yet who can deny that there are other possible origins and inspirations for contemplation?

It is this, I think, that is specially noteworthy in the classical doctrine of contemplation: that the transfiguring experience of divine satiation can come to one in a host of ways. The most trivial of stimuli can bring one to this peak. And this being so, we are brought sharply to the arresting and indeed astounding realization—so opposed is it to everything we are in the habit of thinking about contemporary man—that contemplation is far more widespread among us today than appearances would indicate. The significant features of contemplation can be attained without anyone's being conscious of it by that name. With this as clue, more and more new forms of achieving contemplation manifest themselves.

Let us spend some time on these obscurer varieties of contemplation, even while we omit any discussion of its specifically religious form. Not only is there a highly variegated and distinguished literature on this branch,[9] but I should not feel competent to speak about it in detail. On the other hand, the nature of the other forms of earthly contemplation is such that they acutely want careful thinking through. Or rather, I might even be tempted to say, they need encouragement. For we need to know that the high appreciation accorded for so long to contemplation has every right to be accorded to a good many experiences which come our way in the course of everyday life. And we also need to know that we have a right to take the blessings of such experiences for what they truly are: foretaste and beginning of the perfect joy.[10]

Above all, there is a contemplative way of seeing the things of creation. I am speaking now of actual things, and of seeing with the eyes; I mean also hearing, smelling, tasting, every type of sense-perception, but primarily seeing.

A man drinks at last after being extremely thirsty, and, feeling refreshment permeating his body, thinks and says: What a glorious thing is fresh water! Such a man, whether he knows it or not, has already taken a step toward that "seeing of the beloved object" which is contemplation. How splendid is water, a rose, a tree, an apple, a human face—such exclamations can scarcely be spoken without also giving tongue to an assent and affirmation which extends beyond the object praised and touches upon the origin of the universe. Who among us has not suddenly looked into his child's face, in the midst of the toils and troubles of everyday life, and at that moment "seen" that everything which is good, is loved and lovable, loved by God! Such certainties all mean, at bottom, one and the same thing: that the world is plumb and sound; that everything comes to its appointed goal; that in spite of all appearances, underlying all things is—peace, salvation, *gloria*; that nothing and no one is lost; that "God holds in his hand the beginning, middle, and end of all that is."[11] Such nonrational, intuitive certainties of the divine base of all that is can be vouchsafed to our gaze even when it is turned toward the most insignificant-looking things, if only it is a gaze inspired by love. That, in the precise sense, is contemplation. And we should have the courage to admit its identity.

Out of this kind of contemplation of the created world arise in never-ending wealth all true poetry and all real art, for it is the nature of poetry and art to be paean and praise heard above all the wails of lamentation. No one who is not capable of such contemplation can grasp poetry in a poetic fashion, that is to say, in the only meaningful fashion. The indispensability, the vital function of the arts in man's life, consists above all in this: that through them contemplation of the created world is kept active and alive.

It is well here to speak of the diaries left by Gerard Manley Hopkins.[12] They are filled with testimonies of earthly contemplation; indeed, they speak of little else. This poet, who united dynamic and powerful language with the most refined spiritual perception, devoted passionate attention to the "inscapes" of the visible world—not for the sake of pedantic realistic description, but in order to achieve awareness and obtain possession of the thousandfold riches of the works of God.

Thus he speaks of the flame "brighter and glossier than glass or silk or water" which "reeling up to the right in one long handkerchief and curling like a cartwhip" runs up a heap of dry honeysuckle[13]; of the "burnished or embossed forehead of the sky over the sundown"[14]; of the ridge of a hill "like a pale goldish skin without body"[15]; of the cedar "laying level crow-feather strokes of boughs, with fine wave and dedication in them, against the light"[16]; of a "sleeve of liquid barleyfield."[17] One early morning on the drill ground he catches the "inscape of the horse" which Sophocles had felt and expressed in the choruses "running on the likeness of a horse to a breaker, a wave of the sea curling over."[18] In similar manner he speaks of the Rhone glacier, of the flight of the heron, of young elm leaves, of the peacock's tail; and again and again of the changing shapes of clouds and running water.

The precision of these entries proves, among other things, how little contemplation need bypass or blur the reality of the visible world by, say, premature "symbolization." Rather, contemplation directs its gaze straight at the heart of objects. In so doing, it perceives in the depths a hitherto hidden, nonfinite relationship. And in that perception lies the peculiar essence of contemplation.

But what actually happens when the soul, as it were, takes precedence over the eye? No one has yet succeeded in providing an adequate descriptive account of that process. The flame of the northern lights, blazing in the sky independently of earth's chronology, seeming to "be dated to the day of judgment," fills the enraptured observer "with delightful fear."[19] What was it that was given to him to see? "I do not think I have ever seen anything more beautiful than the bluebell I have been looking at. I know the beauty of the Lord by it."[20] What are the words of the message which has come to him from the heart of flourishing creation? We are not told. For this, too, is part of the nature of contemplation: that it cannot be communicated. It takes place in the innermost recesses. There is no observer. And it is impossible to "set it down" because no energy of the soul is left unengaged.

This passionate precision of sensual description is a demonstration of the intensity with which the gaze of earthly contemplation respects the visible aspects of objects in this world, and tries to preserve them. It would also seem that veneration for concrete reality is kindled by the contemplative impulse which seeks the divine meaning underlying all beings. G. K. Chesterton, considering his life in retrospect, said that he had always had the almost mystical conviction of the miracle in all that exists, and of the rapture dwelling essentially within all experience.[21] Within this statement lie three separate assertions: that everything holds and conceals at bottom a mark of its divine origin; that one who catches a glimpse of it "sees" that this and all things are "good" beyond all comprehension; and that, seeing this, he is happy. Here in sum is the whole doctrine of the contemplation of earthly creation.

XI

It would be astonishing if a host of protests and objections had not been aroused by what has been said so far, levelled not only against this or that point, but against the whole conception. Fairness demands that these criticisms be heard. We shall attempt to meet them squarely.

Exception might be taken in the following terms: Man is above all a creature of action, destined to keep himself alive by his own activities, to make the earth and its natural forces serve him, to establish order in the world by political activity in its widest sense, so that the natural communities of family, nation, and state may be able to live in peace. There are also the labors of peace to be considered: building, construction, achievement of justice by rule and service, mutual aid, active love toward others. What would ethical life be if it were not active fulfillment of duties, discipline of animal vitality, struggle against evil, creation of values? Art, too, after all, is nothing but the production of *poiemata*, of formed structures and works. Even the love of God is not convincing if it fails to be practical. In short, human life means stirring, putting shoulder to the wheel, accomplishing something, laboring, making, working, acting. And in all these things man's happiness also lies; it makes him happy to live in this way.

All this sounds highly plausible; indeed, it gives the impression of being beyond cavil—whereas the statement that man's true happiness and the whole meaning of his life is to be found in contemplation sounds, on the other hand, extremely feeble. At best it may appear an oversophisticated proposition, scarcely meant to be taken literally; an inadmissible generalization, an exaggeration.

What, then, can we say in reply? We must perforce agree. Everything said about man's active nature is, viewed as a whole, incontestably true. It is not only incontestable; it is not contested. Nevertheless, the notion that this stands in contradiction to our doctrine is a delusion. But now the many strands of this argument must be unwoven, and taken up in due order.

Point *one:* Active concern for the preservation of life does demand a large portion of that same life. No one will gainsay this. And obviously, this is not only the fact of the matter; this is how it should be. The human activity which serves this end, and which comprises those phenomena—by now so vast that no one can grasp them all—which we call the economy, production, transportation, technology, and so on—all this cannot simply be dismissed by assignment to the realm of "material things." Rather, the preservation of life is a truly human task which concerns the whole man, which means that it also is subject to the human, which is to say the ethical, norm of life. Very well, what else? Now the disputed point is appearing around the corner. Two questions must be posed: Once the means for living have been obtained, in what will this now-secure life consist? Furthermore, is it not patently absurd to say that the meaning of life consists in securing the means of livelihood? Elementary logic disposes of this last question. But the first question remains open.

Point *two:* At any rate, does not the meaning of life consist in man's being good? But here we must clarify our terms. Do we mean to say that one who does not live justly, courageously, or moderately has missed the meaning of life? If that is the purport, everyone will agree. But what if we are saying that man is here on earth in order to practice these virtues? The ancients insisted on a hierarchy of rank among the virtues; and amazingly enough, they have said that disciplining of the fear of death and of sensual desire (that is, courage and *temperantia*) is not in itself equivalent to "doing good."[1] But what else? The removal of obstacles[2] so that henceforth the really good, that is, the just deed, may be done.

Is, then, justice the purpose of life? Justice is done for the sake of order in the communal life. Is realization of this order fulfilling the purpose of existence? I know that order can never be entirely perfect among men; but here we are not concerned with the succession of things in time, but with their rank and hierarchy. We must recognize that the whole of morality points to something beyond itself; that it makes arrangements for something else; that, in any case, its purpose does not simply lie within itself, and that it therefore cannot constitute the ultimate purpose of life.

But—point *three*—what about active love for our fellow men? What about selfless aid to others? What about works of mercy? Is love not purposeful in itself and therefore the ultimate fulfillment of life? Again, we cannot offer a positive "yes" to this question. One who feeds the hungry primarily wants them to eat their fill. Yet at the same time he must, if he is normal, fervently wish that no one need go hungry—wish, therefore, that there were no reason for him to offer such sustenance. In other words, the purpose of acts of charity lies not within themselves, but in the alleviation of suffering. But what about the concern for the fate of one's fellows out of which such acts sprang? What about the inner affirmation of the existence of others which is the essence of love? Are these not meaningful in themselves? Yes and no. No, because love must necessarily aim at something other than itself. But what do I want if I love someone else? I want him to be happy. In charity, Thomas says, we love others "as companions in the sharing of beatitude."[3] And what is beatitude? Contemplation!

The results we have so far achieved can be summed up as follows: All practical activity, from practice of the ethical virtues to gaining the means of livelihood, serves something other than itself. And this other thing is not practical activity. It is having what is sought after, while we rest content in the results of our active efforts. Precisely that is the meaning of the old adage that the *vita activa* is fulfilled in the *vita contemplativa.*[4] To be sure, the active life contains a felicity of its own; it lies, says Thomas, principally in the practice of prudence, in the perfect art of the conduct of life.[5] But ultimate repose cannot be found in this kind of felicity. *Vita activa est dispositio ad contemplativam*[6]; the ultimate meaning of the active life is to make possible the happiness of contemplation.

In the commentary Thomas wrote on Aristotle's *Nicomachean Ethics* there is a sentence which expresses this idea in so challenging a fashion that I hesitate to cite it here. Thomas is speaking of politics, which is the summation of all man's active cares about securing his existence. The sentence sounds almost utopian. But it is based upon a wholly illusion-free estimate of what is commonly called "political life"; it contains the insight that politics must inevitably become empty agitation if it does not aim at something which is not political. "The whole of political life seems to be ordered with a view to attaining the happiness of contemplation. For peace, which is established and preserved by virtue of political activity, places man in a position to devote himself to contemplation of the truth."[7] Such is the magnificent simplicity and keenness of this dictum that we scarcely dare lean on it. Yet it is nothing but an extension of the idea that contemplation is "the goal of man's whole life."[8]

We do not mean by this to scorn or decry practical life. On the contrary, we may well say that here is the clue to the salvation and redemption of

94

ordinary life. And here it seems proper to put in a word about the nature of hierarchical thinking. The hierarchical point of view admits no doubt about difference in levels and their location; but it also never despises lower levels in the hierarchy. Thus the inherent dignity of practice (as opposed to *theoria*) is in no way denied. It is taken for granted that practice is not only meaningful but indispensable; that it rightly fills out man's weekday life; that without it a truly human existence is inconceivable. Without it, indeed, the *vita contemplativa* is unthinkable.

But practice does become meaningless the moment it sees itself as an end in itself. For this means converting what is by nature a servant into a master —with the inevitable result that it no longer serves any useful purpose. The absurdity and the profound dangers of this procedure cannot, in the long run, remain hidden. André Gide writes in his *Journals:* "The truth is that as soon as we are no longer obliged to earn our living, we no longer know what to do with our life and recklessly squander it."[9] Here, with his usual acuteness, Gide has described the deadly emptiness and the endless ennui which bounds the realm of the exclusively practical like a belt of lunar landscape. This is the desert which results from destruction of the *vita contemplativa*. In the light of such a recognition we suddenly see new and forceful validity in the old principle: "It is requisite for the good of the human community that there should be persons who devote themselves to the life of contemplation."[10] For it is contemplation which preserves in the midst of human society the truth which is at one and the same time useless and the yardstick of every possible use; so it is also contemplation which keeps the true end in sight, gives meaning to every practical act of life.

One exception (point *four*) would seem to be the activity of the artist, which, having nothing to do with either morality or livelihood, is nevertheless a pursuit which triumphantly achieves meaning through perfection of the work of art. Disregarding momentarily the fact that this activity, too, can also and incidentally bring its practitioner his means of livelihood, and that it is always ethical (or antiethical) activity—still the work of art to be perfected cannot be something ultimate. Certainly a work of art has no utilitarian end, and certainly it is not a means to accomplish something else. But may we not ascribe its power to the fact that the process which takes place in the artist takes place also in his audience—who in seeing, hearing, absorbing the work are kindled to contemplation of Creation?

The poet Gottfried Benn, in a significant speech

on growing old, has made a penetrating remark on works of art and their meaning. It contains a statement, and a question which he does not answer. This unanswered question is the chief point. Benn says: "One thing is clear: when something is finished, it must be perfect—but what then?"[11] This is not the tone of someone who thinks a work of art meaningful in itself. To be sure, the question "What then?" is flung into a world that promptly falls mute. "Then" we ought to be able to celebrate, festively commemorate affirmation of the meaning of the world—in the happiness of contemplating something that is not the work of art, but that is brought into view by that work. Perhaps also —in a rare, special case—it should be possible "then" to offer up the completed work as a consecrated gift and sacrifice in the precise meaning of the word. Phidias, when he completed the Athene Promachos, knew the answer to the question "What then?" Bach knew it too, and Bruckner. And probably there is no better answer.

Are we, then, saying that love of God, and all that is done in that name, is the only remaining "activity" which is in itself meaningful? This is—let us recall that we have now reached point *five*—a final element in the counterproposition we are still con-

sidering, one which questions whether contemplation is the ultimate human goal. It seems purely
rhetorical, for who would withhold the affirmative
answer, or venture to contend that it is infinitely
more meaningful to love God than to know Him?
Thomas would not allow himself to be enmeshed
by such verbal snares. If by knowing God the *visio
beatifica* is meant, then what is more meaningful: to
love God or to see Him? If love consists of two
fundamental acts, desiring and joy in possession,[12]
and if knowing is the "noblest form of possession,"[13] can we say that wanting to possess is more
than possession, or that joy is more important than
the reason for joy? In this historical existence, it is
true, in *statu viatoris*—the sages agree on this doctrine—for man here on earth, there is nothing more
meaningful than the love of God, the persistent
striving for "the whole good." But this is so because it may be possible for us to desire God with
our whole beings, but not (not yet!) to possess
Him wholly. Nevertheless, desiring aims at possession. And possession is had in contemplation.

One of the great Greeks before Socrates, Anaxagoras—of whom Aristotle said that he behaved
among his companions like a sober man in a com-
pany of drunks[14]—was asked: To what end are you

in the world? This is the same question with which Christian catechisms begin. Anaxagoras' reply was: *Eis theorian*—in order to behold sun, moon, and sky.[15] This phrase was scarcely intended to refer to the physical heavens. Anaxagoras meant rather the whole of the universe, the whole of being. Thus the cosmological wisdom of the early Greeks and the doctrine of the New Testament, thus Plato and Aristotle, Augustine and Thomas, agree that we partake of the perfection for whose sake we live by *seeing*.

XII

With great sureness of insight, the ancients have asserted that in the contemplative man may be found all the things which distinguish the happy man; and that ordinary speech attributes to both the same characteristics.[1] That, says Thomas, is "quite evident," *manifeste apparet*.[2] What are these identities?

For example there is *simplicitas*, that simplicity peculiar to the gaze of contemplation. The whole energy of the seeing person gathers into a single look.[3] And this having-all-in-one belongs likewise, we are told, to the state of happiness. It seems to me that this is confirmed by our own inner experience. Everything has become utterly simple—this is the cry of a happy person. We might cite here an aphorism of Nietzsche's: "Man's happiness is based upon there being for him an indisputable truth."[4] Here, in cognition, truth and happiness are conjoined under the aspect of simplicity. Disputation involves pros and cons, arguments and counterarguments, variety of points of view, yes and no. But an indisputable truth, not something that is merely not disputed out of mental sluggishness or doggedness, but a truth which is immune even to interior dispute —that is the *simplicitas* of possession.

Furthermore, one of the reasons there can be no perfect beatitude in this physical existence is, says the *Summa Theologica*,[5] that man is not capable of an act continuing without interruption. But happiness is not happiness if it does not endure forever without loss; happiness demands eternity. Nietzsche is full of brilliant comments which might serve as contributions to a phenomenology of happiness. Thus he said it is "always one thing which makes for happiness: . . . the capacity to feel unhistorically."[6] One who is happy steps away from the parcelling up of time and into a reposeful Now, a *nunc stans* in which everything is simultaneous. But this very quality once again links the happy man with the contemplative man. It is not only that the simple insightful gaze of the *intellectus* is related to the "discursive" movements of the *ratio* as the eternal to the temporal.[7] Rather, in contemplation man is capable of remaining longer without fatigue or distraction than in any other activity[8]; time flies by. In happiness as in contemplation, man takes a step out of time.

Seeing, in itself, makes for happiness—and this, too, say the ancients, is a connection between contemplation and happiness. "We prefer seeing to all else"—these words are to be found in the first chapter of Aristotle's *Metaphysics*. If we did not already know that joy in seeing must be counted among the most elemental, irrepressible, coveted joys of mankind, we could deduce it from the everyday phenomenon of "concupiscence of the eyes," the hypertrophy of visual curiosity, the morbidity of the contemporary craving to see. We can deduce it from the extent of this degeneration which, it seems, is imperilling specifically our most elemental and precious powers. . . .[9] This, incidentally, may suggest that the greatest menace to our capacity for contemplation is the incessant fabrication of tawdry empty stimuli which kill the receptivity of the soul. . . .

But we wished to talk about the common features which link the happy and the contemplative man. Another of them is the following: the happy man needs nothing and no one. Not that he holds himself aloof, for indeed he is in harmony with everything and everyone; everything is "in him"; nothing can happen to him. The same may also be said for the contemplative person; he needs himself alone[10]; he lacks nothing; *omnia secum portat.* He lives in a closed sphere. To be precise, he cannot even be disturbed. That was true of Archimedes, who did not notice the conquest of his native Syracuse; it was true also for the Christian martyrs, of whom it is told that not even torture could tear them from the happiness of contemplation.

And finally, repose, leisure, peace, belong among the elements of happiness. If we have not escaped from harried rush, from mad pursuit, from unrest, from the necessity of care, we are not happy. And what of contemplation? Its very premise is freedom from the fetters of workaday busyness. Moreover, it itself actualizes this freedom by virtue of being intuition.

I have recently encountered an unexpected confirmation of this notion, one that is most apropos and completely "modern," founded upon the direct experience of the human heart. I found it in the memoirs of George Santayana, one of the most remarkable and respected philosophers of our times. Santayana relates how he used to accompany a friend versed in art through the great picture galleries of the world. And seeing his friend standing, completely absorbed and enraptured, in front of a masterpiece, he thought and says with great earnestness, and with the clear intent of stating a philosophical thesis: "My own load was lifted, and I saw how instrumental were all the labor and history of man, to be crowned, if crowned at all, only in intuition."[11]

XIII

Anyone who considers the evil in this world with an incorruptible eye and sincere concern may, looking back over the chapters of this book, possibly say: How can we praise contemplation of this earthly creation when the ages, the present age and probably all ages, have been full of disorder, frightful injustice, hunger, painful deaths, oppression, and every form of human misery? Is it possible to keep in mind the actual history of mankind and at the same time speak of the happiness of intuition, of satiation and beatitude? Is this anything but flight from the real world, an attempt to render horrors innocuous, a form of self-deception and unrealistic idyllicism? Ought not a generous person who does not care to deceive himself about what is going on in the world day after day—ought not such a person have the courage to renounce the "escape" of happiness?

This stricture, whose seriousness is immediately evident, can mean several things. We can conceive of a meaning which excludes from the start the possibility of an answer. If behind this renunciation of happiness as an escape lies the conviction that the world is not really plumb and sound; that its dichotomy extends down to the roots; that the speaker does not accept the world as it is; that he withholds his consent—if this is what is meant, then discussion is impossible. Or more precisely, discussion would necessarily involve so many antecedent positions that we cannot begin on it here. I do not say that such a view—which by the way is by no means rare nowadays—cannot coincide with high-mindedness; it can even be combined quite emphatically with an attitude of active helpfulness (although this is a case of happy inconsistency). But no one who thinks of the world as at bottom unredeemable can accept the idea that contemplation is the supreme happiness of man. Neither happiness nor contemplation is possible except on the basis of consent to the world as a whole. This consent has little to do with "optimism." It is a consent that may be granted amid tears and the extremes of horror.

If, accordingly, everything that has been said in this book rests upon the presumption that in the final analysis all is right with the world, that everything created is loved by God, that there is an Eternal Life, and that happiness is *aliquid divinissimum,* "something utterly divine"[1]—then it must not be forgotten for a moment that this is a pure gift. We are not responsible for its being so. It is no merit of ours that the possibility of happiness exists. Indeed, we might say that it exists in spite of us. May not, incidentally, a sense of shame at being the recipient of so immeasurable a gift be an unconscious factor behind the refusal of consent outlined above? On the other hand, there exists also the determination to accept nothing as a gift. However, the motive force underlying the lives of quite a few saints has been that same sense of shame, the ashamed insight that we ought to "merit" the gift of happiness.

Further: The teachers of Western Christianity have one and all agreed that the imperfect contemplation of this earth is an *inchoatio vitae aeternae*, a foretaste of Eternal Beatitude.[2] This states the crucial fact about earthly contemplation, but by no means tells the whole story. It would be a crude misunderstanding to consider the *vita contemplativa* sheer pleasure. The happiness of contemplation is not a comfortable happiness. The great Spanish mystic, Teresa of Avila, has asserted that more courage is required to lead a life of contemplation than to elect martyrdom.[3] And the references to the "dark night" recur time and again in all spiritual doctrines of the *vita contemplativa;* this, it would seem, is an inescapable phase of the contemplative life.

Earthly contemplation means to the Christian, we have said, this above all: that behind all that we directly encounter the Face of the incarnate Logos becomes visible. This is not meant in any gnostic and mythical sense. Rather, we mean something simultaneously superhistorical and historical. The historical element is this: that the Face of the Divine Man bears the marks of a shameful execution. Contemplation does not ignore the "historical Gethsemane," does not ignore the mystery of evil, guilt and its bloody atonement. The happiness of contemplation is a true happiness, indeed the supreme happiness; but it is founded upon sorrow. "Delightful fear," says Gerard Manley Hopkins.[4] "Fear with joy the Last Judgment."[5]

Earthly contemplation is imperfect contemplation. In the midst of its repose there is unrest. This unrest stems from man's experiencing at one and the same moment the overwhelming infinitude of the object, and his own limitations. It is part of the nature of earthly contemplation that it glimpses a light whose fearful brightness both blesses and dazzles.

"Contemplation does not rest until it has found the object which dazzles it."

NOTES

The motto by Konrad Weiss is taken from a posthumous fragment which I have had the opportunity to read through the kindness of Frau Maria Weiss. The title of this fragment, which Weiss reworked no less than nine times in the course of a decade, is *On Poverty in the Spirit*.

Key to Abbreviations

The quotations from St. Thomas's *Summa Theologica* are indicated in the notes only by numerals. (For example, "II, II, 150, 1 ad 2" means: "Part II of Section II, quaestio 150, articulus 1, reply to the second objection.") The same method is used for references to the commentary on the *Sentences* of Peter Lombard. (Example: "2d. 24, 3, 5" means: "Book 2, distinctio 24, quaestio 3, articulus 5.") The titles of the other works of St. Thomas cited in the text are abbreviated as follows:

C.G.   = *Summa contra Gentes*
Ver.   = *Quaestiones disputatae de veritate*
Pot.   = *Quaestiones disputatae de potentia Dei*
Mal.   = *Quaestiones disputatae de malo*
Car.   = *Quaestio disputata de caritate*
Virt. comm. = *Quaestio disputata de virtutibus in communi*

Quol.   = *Quaestiones quodlibetales*
Comp. theol. = *Compendium theologiae*
In Joh.   = *Commentary on the Gospel of St. John*
In Met.   = *Commentary on Aristotle's Metaphysics*
In Eth.   = *Commentary on Aristotle's Nicomachean Ethics*
In De causis = *Commentary on the Liber de causis*
In Hebdom.   = *Commentary on Boethius' Essay on Axioms* (*De hebdomadibus*)

I

1 Manifesto of the PEN Club, 1951.
2 *Ultima hominis felicitas* [*est*] *in contemplatione veritatis.* C.G. 3, 37.
3 Thomas in the *Summa contra Gentes* always speaks of *beatitudo* when he means *divine* happiness; when, on the other hand, he speaks in the third book of human happiness—meaning always man's *eternal* bliss—he uses almost exclusively the word *felicitas: In illa felicitate, quae provenit ex visione divina* . . . (C.G. 3, 63). In his *Commentary on the Nicomachean Ethics*, too, he uses exclusively *felicitas.* But curiously enough, in the second part of the *Summa Theologica* (I, II, 2-5), written at almost the same time, he regularly uses the word *beatitudo* in the same sense.
4 *Sicut bonum creatum est quaedam similitudo et participatio boni increati, ita adeptio boni creati est quaedam similitudinaria beatitudo.* Mal. 5, 1 ad 5.
5 *Le terrible, c'est qu'on ne peut jamais se griser suffisamment. Journal,* 1889-1939 (Paris, 1948), p. 89.
6 *Purgatorio,* Canto 27.

II

1 *Non enim bruta possunt dici felicia nisi abusive.* C.G. 3, 27.

2 I, 94, 1.

3 C.G. 4, 92; similarly I, II, 13, 6.

4 I, 19, 10.

5 I, 82, 1 ad 3.

6 I, II, 69, 1; I, II, 3, 1.

7 *Tale bonum, quod voluntas non potest non velle, quod est beatitudo* . . . I, II, 10, 2.

8 I, 41, 2; C.G. 1, 50.

9 C.G. 3, 100.

10 I, 41, 2 ad 3.

11 I, II, 6, 1 ad 3.

12 *Voluntas libere appetit felicitatem, licet necessario appetat illam.* Pot. 10, 2 ad 5.

13 204e-205a (Jowett translation).

14 Kant, *Critique of Practical Reason.*

15 Kant, *Foundations of the Metaphysic of Ethics.*

16 Kant, *Critique of Practical Reason.*

17 2 d. 38, 1, 2 ad 2.

18 192 c-d (Jowett translation).

19 "We ought to make ourselves happy; that is the true morality." Kant, *Lecture on Ethics.*

20 *De vita beata,* cap. 4. In this connection we must once again quote from Immanuel Kant: "Man's greatest good fortune is that he himself is the author of his felicity, when he feels he is enjoying that which he himself has won." *Lecture on Ethics.*

21 Cap. 25.

22 In Eth. 1, 10; no. 129.

23 *Aliquis dicitur viator ex eo, quod tendit in beatitudi-*
   nem; comprehensor autem dicitur ex eo, quod iam
   beatitudinem obtinet. III, 15, 10.

24 I, 62, 4.

III

1 In Part One of the *Summa Theologica* there is an entire *quaestio* which treats *De divina beatitudine* (I,
  26); it forms the conclusion of the theology. Likewise,
  the first book of the *Summa contra Gentes* concludes
  with three chapters on the beatitude of God (1, 100-
  102).

2 C.G. 1, 101.

3 C.G. 1, 101.

4 2 d. 15, 3, 3 ad 1.

5 Cf. Hermann Volk, *Gott lebt und gibt Leben* (Munich, 1953), pp. 40f.

6 Paul Claudel in a letter to Jacques Rivière, October
  24, 1907.

IV

1 I, II, 5, 8.

2 *Finis dupliciter dicitur scil. ipsa res, quam adipisci*
  desideramus, et usus seu adeptio vel possessio illius rei.
  I, II, 2, 7.

3 This corresponds to the academic distinction between
  "objective" and "subjective" ("formal") happiness.

4 *Id in quo beatitudo consistit et quod beatum facit . . .*
  est aliquid extra animam. I, II, 2, 7.

5 *Sermones,* no. 156, 7.

6 *Epist. Moral.* XI, 2 (no. 19f.).

7 *City of God,* 19, 1.

8 C.G. 3, 26-63; I, II, 2-5; In Eth. 10, 9-12. We must also mention here the three-volume work by the Spanish Dominican, J. M. Ramírez, *De hominis beatitudine* (Madrid, 1942-1947). I am much indebted to this unusually thorough and independent commentary on St. Thomas's doctrine of beatitude.

9 I, II, 2, 1. This concept develops an idea found in Aristotle's *Politics,* 1, 8f.

10 *Appetitus divitiarum artificialium est infinitus.* I, II, 2, 1 ad 3.

11 "Real happiness is nothing but the happiness of existing, or: existing is in itself happiness." D. Sternberger, *Figuren der Fabel,* (Frankfurt, 1950) p. 168.

12 I, II, 2, 5.

13 C.G. 3, 29.

14 In Eth. 1, 18; no. 219. Highly worth noting is the addendum: ". . . Just as in the realm of cognition the primary principles are not known, but more than known, namely intuited."

15 Thomas quotes the traditional definition: *gloria est clara notitia cum laude.* I, II, 2, 3.

16 *Confessiones,* 13, 38. *De Trinitate,* 6, 10.

17 *Bonum hominis dependet sicut ex causa ex cognitione Dei, et ideo ex gloria, quae est apud Deum, dependet beatitudo hominis sicut ex causa sua.* I, II, 2, 3.

18 I, II, 2, 4.

19 Cicero, *De oratore,* 1, 1.

20 II, II, 150, 1 ad 1.

21 I, II, 2, 8.

22 *Nihil potest quietare voluntatem hominis nisi bonum universale.* I, II, 2, 8.

23 Thus Kierkegaard in *Sickness unto Death.* More on this idea in Josef Pieper, *Leisure the Basis of Culture* (Pantheon, 1952), pp. 49ff.; also *Über die Hoffnung,* pp. 6off.

24 . . . *bonum universale, quod non invenitur in aliquo creato, sed solum in Deo. . . . Unde solus Deus voluntatem hominis implere potest.* I, II, 2, 8.

25 *Cum ergo homo non sit capax boni, quod excedit limites totius creaturae, videtur quod per aliquod bonum creatum homo beatus fieri possit.* I, II, 2, 8, obi. 3.

26 I, II, 2, 8 ad 3.

V

1 Cf. Josef Pieper, *Was heisst akademisch?* (Munich, 1952), p. 76ff.

2 I, II, 4, 1; 4, 5 ad 5.

3 In Eth. 1, 13; no. 161.

4 C.G. 3, 26.

5 I, II, 2, 6.

6 I, II, 2, 7.

7 *Videre, recordari, scire, virtutem habere.* In Eth. 10, 4; no. 2003. This list follows that of Aristotle (*Nic. Ethics,* 10, 2; 1174 a).

8 In Eth. 10, 4; no. 2003.

9 I, II, 2, 6 obi. 1.

10 I, II, 2, 6 ad 1.

11 *Sic delectatio est appetibilis propter aliud, id est prop-*
ter bonum, quod est delectationis obiectum. I, II, 2, 6
ad 1.

12 *Ex modo omnes appetunt delectationes, sicut et appe-*
tunt bonum; et tamen delectationem appetunt ratione
boni, et non e converso. . . . *Unde non sequitur quod*
delectatio sit maximum et per se bonum; sed quod una-
quaeque delectatio consequatur aliquod bonum, et
aliqua delectatio consequatur id quod est per se et
maximum bonum. I, II, 2, 6 ad 3.

VI

1 This aphorism, which might almost derive from one
of the sages of the Orient, is evidently a contemporary
coinage. I do not know the author.

2 *Beatitudo consistit in uno eodem active, in Deo; pas-*
sive in anima . . . *Beatitudo* . . . *consistit in recep-*
tione. Sermones de tempore, 9 and 11.

3 I, II, 3, 1.

4 "Bliss is a feeling"—this is the thesis of a small posthumous essay by Theodor Haecker, *Metaphysik des*
Fühlens (Munich, 1950). The argument is weakened
from the start by a fundamental misunderstanding of
the Augustinian *analogia Trinitatis (memoria—intel-*
lectus—voluntas).

5 "In so far as man's beatitude is something created
which has existence in himself, it must necessarily be
said that man's beatitude is an activity [*operatio*]."
I, II, 3, 2. "Even God Himself would not be happy if
He did not know and love." Ver. 29, 1.

6 Bartholomé de Medina on Thomas I, II, 3, 2 (cited in Ramírez, III, p. 76).

7 "Beatitude is man's supreme perfection." I, II, 3, 2.

8 "Every being is perfected to the degree that it is actualized [*actu*]." I, II, 3, 2.

9 I, II, 3, 2.

10 *Operatio est ultimus actus operantis.* I, II, 3, 2.

11 Here we refer to the distinction common among the Scholastics: *actus primus—actus secundus.* "First reality" is actual existence, whereas "second reality" implies that this actually existing being realizes its potentialities by being active. *Operatio est actus secundus operantis* (I, II, 70, 1); and: *actus secundus est perfectior quam actus primus* (C.G. 1, 45).

12 I, II, 3, 2 ad 3.

13 Cf. Ramírez, III, p. 78.

14 I, II, 3, 2 ad 3.

15 I, 27, 1.

16 I, 27, 1.

17 Konrad Weiss in a letter to Katharina Kippenberg (August 14, 1939).

VII

1 *Essentia beatitudinis in actu intellectus consistit.* I, II, 3, 4.

2 Duns Scotus thought he detected in this sentence a quotation from the works of Anselm of Canterbury. Compare on this point P. Rousselot, *L'Intellectualisme de Saint Thomas* (Paris, 1936), p. 48.

3 Migne, *Patrologia Latina*, 175, 1065.

4 I, II, 3, 4.

5 *Manifeste apparet* . . . I, II, 3, 4. *Manifeste ostenditur* . . . C.G. 3, 26.

6 Augustine, *De Trinitate*, 13, 5.

7 I, II, 3, 4, obi. 5.

8 I, II, 3, 4 ad 5.

9 . . . *quod quidem est per aliud quam per actum voluntatis.* I, II, 3, 4 ad 5.

10 Bartolomé de Medina (cited in Ramírez, III, 176).

11 For example, E. Gilson maintains that Augustine in his doctrine of beatitude defends the "primacy of the will." *Introduction à l'étude de S. Augustin* (Paris, 1929), pp. 1-11. On the other hand F. Cayré (*La Contemplation Augustienne*, Paris, 1929, pp. 251f.) speaks of Augustine's "intellectualism," which did not permit him to think of the dictum "God is love" apart from that other dictum, "God is light."

12 *Nihil aliud est habere quam nosse. Eighty-three Questions,* 35, 1.

13 Ibid., 33, 1.

14 In *Psalmos*, 90, 2.

15 *Sermones,* 302 (Migne, *Patrologia Latina,* 39, 2324); also *De Trinitate,* 1, 9. Thomas, too, cites this sentence frequently, for example: Ver. 14, 5 ad 5; Quol. 8, 19, obi. 3.

16 Rousselot, *L'Intellectualisme,* p. xvi.

17 "*L'intellection* . . . *est, pour S. Thomas, essentiellement captatrice d'être et non fabrication d'énoncés.*" Rousselot, *L'Intellectualisme,* p. xvii.

18 In *De causis,* 18; similarly, 4 d. 49, 3, 5, 1 ad 2.

19 I, 14, 1.

20 Ver. 2, 2.
21 *On the Soul*, 3, 8; 431 b.
22 In Met. 12, 8; no. 2544. Rousselot calls knowing *"action vitale par excellence."* *L'Intellectualisme*, p. 7.

VIII

1 I, II, 3, 4.
2 *Ultimus . . . finis hominis est id, quod est primo desideratum. Non autem potest esse quod primo volitum sit actus voluntatis.* Quol. 8, 19.
3 *Multo minus motus est finis . . .* Comp. theol., 1, 107.
4 I, 81, 1.
5 *Oportet igitur aliquid aliud esse quam actum voluntatis, per quod fit finis praesens voluntati.* I, II, 3, 4.
6 Helmut Gollwitzer, *Dying We Live* (Pantheon, 1956).
7 For example, Gen. 4:1; 4:17; 4:25; Luke 1:34.
8 "This is evidently the original meaning of the Hebrew verb 'to know': to be in immediate contact with." Martin Buber, *Bilder von Gut und Böse*, p. 24.
9 3 d. 35, 1, 2, 1.
10 *Sans l'amour la contemplation n'existerait pas.* H. A. Montagne, *La Contemplation mystique. Revue thomiste*, 2 (1919), p. 90.

IX

1 Ludwig Kerstiens, *Cognitio speculativa. Untersuchung zur Geschichte und Bedeutung des Begriffes*

vor und bei Thomas von Aquin. 1951. (Unprinted dissertation.)

2 *Intellectus et ratio differunt quantum ad modum cognoscendi, quia scil. intellectus cognoscit simplici intuitu, ratio vero discurrendo de uno in aliud.* I, 59, 1 ad 1.

3 *Certitudo rationis est ex intellectu; sed necessitas rationis est ex defectu intellectus.* II, II, 49, 5 ad 1. *Ex imperfectione intellectualis naturae provenit ratiocinativa cognitio.* C.G. 1, 57 (8).

4 *Manifestum est quod defectivus quidam intellectus est ratio.* C.G. 1, 57 (8).

5 Dietrich von Hildebrand, *Umgestaltung in Christus* (Einsiedeln, 1950), p. 88.

6 In Joh. 1:1. Thomas von Aquin, *Das Wort* (Kösel Verlag, Munich, 1955), p. 27.

7 Garrigou-Lagrange, Reginald, *Christian Perfection and Contemplation* (B. Herder, St. Louis, 1937). *Prima et maxima contemplatio est admiratio maiestatis.* Bernard of Clairvaux, *De consideratione*, Book 5, last chapter. *Admiratio est actus consequens contemplationem sublimis veritatis.* II, II, 180, 3 ad 3.

8 C.G. 4, 33.

9 Paul Claudel in a letter to Jacques Rivière, May 23, 1907.

X

1 *Tam Dei quam angeli quam etiam hominis ultima felicitas et beatitudo Dei contemplatio est, non solum*

secundum sanctos, sed etiam secundum philosophos. 2
d. 4, 1.

2 *Felicitas humana non consistit in cognitione Dei, quae
habetur per demonstrationem.* C.G. 3, 39. This sentence is the heading of the chapter.

3 C.G. 3, 40.

4 *Per cognitionem autem fidei non fit res credita intel-
lectui praesens perfecte, quia fides de absentibus est,
non de praesentibus.* C.G. 3, 40.

5 I, II, 3, 5.

6 In Eth. 10, 12; no. 2125. Wilhelm Szilasi in his inter-
pretations of Plato and Aristotle has expressed the
same idea from the *Nicomachean Ethics*, which
Thomas takes up here, in the following manner: "The
happy outcome of *theoria* is human happiness."
(*Macht und Ohnmacht des Geistes*, Freiburg 1947, p.
154.)

7 Cf. Josef Pieper, *Leisure the Basis of Culture* (Pantheon, 1952).

8 "Love of God, in so far as He is blessed and the author
of beatitude"—that, says Thomas (Car. 2 ad 8), is the
essence of *caritas*. *Caritas non est qualiscumque amor
Dei, sed amor Dei, quo diligitur ut beatitudinis obiectum.* I, II, 65, 5 ad 1. Similarly, II, II, 23, 1; Car. 7.

9 I shall mention only: Garrigou-Lagrange, *Christian
Perfection and Contemplation* (B. Herder, St. Louis
1937); Dietrich von Hildebrand, *Umgestaltung in
Christus* (Einsiedeln, 1950); Hans-Urs von Balthasar,
Das betrachtende Gebet (Einsiedeln, 1955).

10 *Per eam (contemplationem) fit nobis quaedam in-*

choatio beatitudinis, quae hic incipit, ut in futuro con-tinuetur. II, II, 180, 4.

11 Plato, *Laws*, 715 e.

12 *The Notebooks and Papers of Gerard Manley Hopkins*, edited with notes and preface by Humphrey House (Oxford University Press, London and New York, 1937).

13 P. 159.

14 P. 133.

15 P. 181.

16 P. 185.

17 P. 181.

18 P. 189.

19 P. 135.

20 Pp. 134f.

21 Maisie Ward, *Gilbert Keith Chesterton* (Sheed & Ward, London & New York).

XI

1 II, II, 157, 4.

2 II, II, 123, 12.

3 Car. 7.

4 II, II, 182, 4.

5 *Felicitas contemplativa nihil aliud est quam perfecta contemplatio summae veritatis; felicitas autem activa est actus prudentiae, quo homo se et alios gubernat.* Virt. comm. 5 ad 8; Ver. 14, 2.

6 3 d. 35, 1, 3, 3.

7 In Eth. 10, 11; no. 2102.

8 II, II, 180, 4.

9 *La vérité, c'est que, dès que le besoin d'y subvenir ne nous oblige plus, nous ne savons que faire de notre vie, et que nous la gâchons au hasard. Journal 1889-1939* (Paris, 1948), p. 394.

10 4 d. 26, 1, 2.

11 Gottfried Benn, *Altern als Problem für Künstler. Merkur*, 1954, p. 316.

12 II, II, 3, 4.

13 In *De causis*, 18.

14 *Metaphysik*, 1, 3; 984 b.

15 *Diogenes Laertius*, II, 10.

XII

1 Cf. Ramírez, III, pp. 204ff.

2 In Eth. 10, 11; no. 2103.

3 II, II, 180, 3; In Hebdom., prolog.

4 *Die Unschuld des Werdens* (posthumous works), I (Kröner Edition), p. 84.

5 I, II, 3, 2 ad 4.

6 *Vom Nutzen und Nachteil der Historie für das Leben. Unzeitgemässe Betrachtungen* (Kröner Edition), p. 103.

7 C.G. 2, 96.

8 In Eth. 10, 10; no. 2088f.

9 II, II, 141, 2 ad 2. Cf. also Josef Pieper, *Fortitude and Temperance* (Pantheon, 1954).

10 In Eth. 10, 10; no. 2095; 10, 12; no. 2119ff.

11 George Santayana, *The Middle Span* (New York, 1945), p. 142.

1 In Eth. 1, 14; no. 169.
2 II, II, 180, 4.
3 *Das Leben der heiligen Theresia von Jesu, von ihr selbst beschrieben* (Munich, 1933), p. 304.
4 See Section X, end.
5 Concluding line of the poem, *Fürchte Gott*, by Elisabeth Langgässer, published in *Der Torso* (Hamburg, 1947), p. 90.